. . . the ultimate self-help book. It's thorough and concise and combines all elements necessary for a person wanting to improve the quality of his or her life.

—Dr. Nancy Bonus, Founder/Developer of The Bonus
Plan Non-Diet Weight Loss Program

From Sabotage to Success is medicine for the soul. It's one of those 'I couldn't put it down' experiences that only happens rarely. The saying 'You only get out of it what you put into it' truly applies to this dynamic tool for inner healing and freeing the soul to soar to unlimited heights. I will share this handbook with my clients and students when I recognize the symptoms of sabotage that are identified within.

—Rev. Dr. Ahman, founder of Inspirations Ministries
based in Long Beach, CA., and author of *The
Dynamics of the Spiritual Mind Treatment* and *Healing Fear*

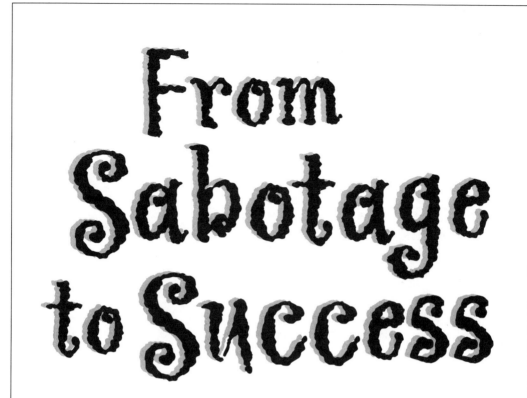

From Sabotage to Success

How to Overcome Self-Defeating Behavior and Reach Your True Potential

Sheri O. Zampelli

NEW HARBINGER PUBLICATIONS, INC.

Distributed in the U.S.A. by Publishers Group West; in Canada by Raincoast Books; in Great Britain by Airlift Book Company, Ltd.; in South Africa by Real Books, Ltd.; in Australia by Boobook; and in New Zealand by Tandem Press.

Copyright © 2000 by Sheri O. Zampelli
New Harbinger Publications, Inc.
5674 Shattuck Avenue
Oakland, CA 94609

Cover design by Poulson/Gluck Design
Cover illustration by Tim Teebken
Author photo by Wolf J. Poltl
Edited by Angela Watrous
Text design by Tracy Marie Powell

Library of Congress Catalog Card Number: 99-75277
ISBN 1-57224-181-0 Paperback

Sheri O. Zampelli's Web site address: www.sabotagetosuccess.com
New Harbinger Publications' Web site address: www.newharbinger.com

02   01   00

10   9   8   7   6   5   4   3   2   1

First printing

This book is dedicated to my grandma Bette Olson. Your love and support fed my soul. I miss you so much, but you're forever a part of me.

Contents

to live, I'm afraid to die, I'm afraid of everything in between."
✳ Focusing on Negatives—"What if things don't work out?"
✳ Unworthiness—"I'm not good enough, I'm not important."
✳ Impatience—"I want it all, and I want it now." ✳ Need for Validation—"I want everyone to like me." ✳ Task List and Action Plan ✳ Summary of Self-Defeating Attitudes ✳ Your Top Ten Self-Defeating Attitudes, Beliefs, and Feelings

a Learning Tool ✳ Focus on the Facts ✳ Written Dialogue: Changing Your Perspective ✳ Say Good-bye to Self-Sabotage ✳ Task List and Action Plan ✳ Writing an Effective Affirmation ✳ Affirmation Tracking Worksheet ✳ Root Down Worksheet

Acknowledgments

I'd like to thank my workshop participants who were bold enough to ask questions, share stories, and disagree with me from time to time. They have made a tremendous contribution to this book and its contents. Thank you Alice Potter for lovingly pointing out my self-defeating behavior and believing in my potential to succeed. Thank you, John Fylppa and Pat McKean at Long Beach City College, for believing in me and offering your support.

Thank you, Dr. Nancy Bonus, for helping me break free from my food compulsions and introducing me to eye-opening and mind-expanding concepts. Thank you to Susan Jeffers, Ph.D., for kindly answering my questions and leading me in the right direction. Your time and patience have not gone unnoticed. Thank you to Carolyn Lee, Harold Nebenzal, and Paul Leserman for doing extra footwork on my behalf.

Thank you to my husband for loving me as I am and creating a safe space for the real me to grow. Thank you to twelve-step programs for teaching me about recovery and change. Thank you to Mariposa Women's Center for creating a space for my workshops. Thank you, Jassamine Thornburgh, for your creative input.

Introduction

What is familiar is comfortable, even if it's unhealthy or self-defeating. We're familiar with our lifelong negative attitudes and behaviors, and this familiarity breeds a sense of comfort. It's safer and easier to handle the negative self-talk than it is to challenge it, even though it intensifies feelings of fear, insecurity, and low self-esteem. When we begin changing our attitudes and behaviors, it feels uncomfortable in the beginning because it is unfamiliar. With time, however, your new way of relating to the world becomes more comfortable and familiar.

Resistance is a normal part of change. You're not "bad," "wrong," "sick," or "crazy" just because you resist change. Everyone is afraid of change. In her book *Feel the Fear and Do It Anyway*, Dr. Susan Jeffers states these five basic truths about fear:

1. Fear will never go away as long as you continue to grow.

2. The only way to get rid of your fear of doing something is to go out and do it.

3. The only way to feel better about yourself is to go out and do it (don't wait to feel better and *then* do something).

4. Not only are you going to experience fear every time you are in unfamiliar territory, so will everyone else.

5. Pushing through fear is less frightening than living with the bigger, underlying fear that comes from a feeling of helplessness.

In order to be open to change, it's important to accept yourself exactly as you are right now. Try not to beat yourself up for sabotaging yourself, because that will just make you less resistant to further self-sabotage. If you sabotage yourself because you don't believe you deserve good things, beating yourself up is just reinforcing that you're no good, and that's counterproductive to your goals. Why not begin your self-change now by congratulating yourself for purchasing this book. Put the critic away so you can have an open, receptive mind to the ideas and concepts that follow. You've made an important step in your self-change today. Future changes will be much easier to make if you let go of self-criticism and forgive yourself for your past mistakes.

Try to keep an open mind as you read this book. Many of the exercises presented in the upcoming chapters may be familiar to you. Perhaps you've already done them or you have a preconceived notion that "they won't work." I encourage you to try all of the exercises, customizing them to suit your personality. I've done every single exercise outlined in this book. Some worked better than others for me personally, but *none* of them made my life worse. There is nothing in this book that will harm you. Open yourself to change by making a commitment to yourself to do the exercises.

I use stories in this book to help illustrate certain points. Some of these examples won't apply specifically to you, but I encourage you to read them all. Rather than looking at the specifics of a story, try to look for the underlying principles. Finally, know that there is no perfect way to read this book or to do the exercises within. As the final chapter will show, quitting is the only way to fail. Whatever you do, don't give up and you will always be a success.

Why I Wrote This Book

I wrote this book out of frustration and a quest for solutions. It's the book I needed many years ago, providing step-by-step help to overcome self-defeating behaviors. In this book, I have compiled all of the tools that I and many others have used to overcome self-defeating behaviors.

Ten years ago, I had no desire to write a self-help book. In fact, I was hesitant to read one. I was convinced that all those success people were a bunch of phonies out to get my money. I was sure that they had never struggled or strained in life and I indignantly thought, "Who are they to tell me to change my attitude?"

I have the classic history of a self-saboteur. I grew up in a dysfunctional home where sexual, physical, and emotional abuse were part of life. We moved on a regular basis and I never formed a long-term friendship. We had little money. In hopelessness and despair I turned to drugs and drinking. My powerlessness turned inward and I felt like a failure. By the time I was seventeen, I was shooting heroin on a daily basis.

Being loaded led to a variety of poor choices. I dropped out of high school and moved out of the house at sixteen. I eventually became homeless. At the age of eighteen I began attending twelve-step meetings. I finally got clean three years later, but not until I failed at two recovery programs and attempted suicide.

Quitting drugs helped me, but it didn't solve my problems. The two main reasons I used drugs were to stay thin and to avoid my painful feelings. Once I quit drugs, the feelings, and the weight, were back. I became a compulsive, out-of-control binge eater.

Staying clean reawakened my dreams and desires. I'd always wanted a college education, but my self-worth was so low that I doubted I could succeed. My first semester of school seemed too easy. I liked the A's I was getting on the one hand, but on the other hand I knew I didn't deserve them. I felt I had to suffer to succeed. I couldn't accept the fact that I might actually be smart. When it looked like I might get A's in all my classes, I "forgot" to turn in a paper so that my grade could be lowered. I was terrified to think that I might be placed on the honor roll. My name did not belong there. In another class I slept through my final, ensuring that I would fail the class.

I started to read books about self-sabotage and they only made me feel worse. They would explain the reasons people self-sabotage, list the types of behaviors that are self-defeating, and show how self-sabotage is related to dysfunctional upbringings. I kept waiting for the good part where the book would tell me what I could do to change, but it never came. I identified with the stories, but it only made me feel categorized and hopeless. I couldn't change how I was raised. My childhood was over. I felt like I had no choice but to stay miserable my whole life.

Eventually, my frustration was great enough that I searched desperately for help. My compulsive overeating was worse than ever. I was at the point that I didn't care about being thin anymore, I just wanted to stop feeling crazy. In desperation I tried a nondiet weight loss plan developed by Dr. Nancy Bonus. She was the first person to tell me that my beliefs were creating my reality, and that if I wanted to change the outside, I had to start on the inside. I started using positive affirmations to deal with my weight and body image issues—and the results were spectacular. I realized that if affirmations worked on weight and eating issues, they would work in other areas as well.

I began facilitating workshops on overcoming self-sabotage in 1992. The more I studied the nature of self-sabotage and met people who sabotaged their own success, the more I felt the need for a new kind of book addressing self-sabotage. Many people felt a sense of hope after learning new ways to deal with self-sabotage. They now had a course of action to follow that really worked, and they didn't feel trapped in a cycle of self-defeating behavior. As I facilitated the workshops, I too increased my feelings of hope. I continued to build my confidence and wanted to share the message of hope with a wider audience. When I decided I wanted to write a book that would address overcoming self-sabotage, I had to do some work first. I had to overcome thoughts like, "Who do you think you are to write a book?" "Why would anyone want to read a book written by you?" and "What if the book sucks? Everyone is going to make fun of you." I also had to build up enough experience using the techniques outlined in this book that I would feel comfortable sharing them with you.

Regardless of the depths of your own self-defeating behavior, the principles outlined in this book can help you to overcome the thoughts and feelings that lead to self-defeat. You can increase your level of self-esteem and learn to look at old situations in new, empowering ways.

I have used every technique in this book. I've filled out every worksheet. I've attempted to make this book as down-to-earth and user-friendly as possible. Since I started using these techniques my self-esteem has improved drastically. I have only scratched the surface of my potential, but I know that if I can go from where I was to where I am now, anything is possible. I tell you my story in hopes that you will feel that change is possible for you, too. I still have a background of abuse, pain, and insecurity, but I'm not letting that hold me back anymore. I can't change the past, but I can change today and tomorrow. You can, too. I hope to see you on the road to success.

1

Sabotage Versus Success

What Is Self-Sabotage?

Michael sells real estate. He's a great salesperson, but once he realizes he's about to close a deal he's frozen by fear and occasionally loses customers. Rachel lost her job two years ago. She spends most of her day at home alone. She has developed a habit of pulling out her own hair that has become so severe that she has permanent bald spots. Christopher has met the woman of his dreams three times. He enjoys meeting women and is quite a romantic; however, every time things start to get serious, he runs away. Stephanie is a talented artist. She has been given many opportunities, but continually loses important phone numbers or arrives hours late for important appointments. She makes a strong resolve to change, but repeatedly does things to undermine her progress.

What do these four people have in common? They all engage in self-sabotage. Self-sabotage is an accumulation of thoughts, feelings, and actions that create a road-block to success. Persons who engage in self-sabotage tend to deny themselves pleasure or undermine good feelings. We're often attracted to unhealthy relationships and tend to deny help from others. People who self-sabotage often find a loving, supportive mate "boring." Instead, we may choose unreliable, untrustworthy people to have in our lives. Many people who identify with self-sabotage also report feelings of unworthiness or not being good enough. Others feel guilty about positive events or fail to complete important tasks on time.

In his book *Don't Shoot Yourself in the Foot,* Daniel G. Amen lists the hallmarks of self-sabotage, outlining the differences between sabotage and success in attitudes and behaviors. The following table gives an overall view of his findings.

Sabotaging Behavior	Successful Behavior
lack of personal responsibility	taking personal responsibility
negative attitudes	setting and working toward goals
lack of awareness	taking initiative to be informed
inability to communicate effectively	communicating with others in a positive manner
inability to make wise choices in life	making wise choices about what goes in your mind and body

According to research, people with self-defeating behavior were likely to have been raised in homes that were to some degree unloving, inconsistent, or unpredictable: "People scoring higher on the scale of self-defeating personality perceived their family environments as lacking cohesiveness. Men also perceived their family environments as discouraging open expression of feelings, being unconcerned about school and work achievement, and providing no ethical or religious values" (Schill et al. 1991). Many people who self-sabotage report feeling unappreciated or in some way neglected by their parents: "People who had more characteristics of self-defeating personality were more likely to recall ambivalent and avoidance attachment histories regarding their mothers. There was a tendency for men to recall avoidance attachment histories for fathers as well" (Williams and Schill 1993). If this is your truth, you don't have to continue this cycle in adulthood. You can learn to be loving and consistent. You can learn to appreciate yourself. Depriving yourself of happiness is a form of self-abuse and self-neglect. You may currently be doing to yourself what your parents unjustly did to you, but you are not powerless over change. You can learn positive steps to retrain yourself and break self-defeating habits.

Focusing on childhood experiences can be helpful in identifying deep-seated issues; however, these issues are sometimes used as an excuse to avoid change and rationalize self-sabotage. Each of us is responsible for breaking the cycle of abuse in our own lives. We do this by deciding not to abuse ourselves anymore. There are many forms of self-abuse, including denying yourself special items or denying basic needs such as sleep, proper nutrition, or exercise. It might be denying your own interests and dreams in favor of making money or pleasing others. A common form of self-sabotage is making verbal assaults on ourselves. When asked to outline the self-talk preceding self-sabotage, my workshop participants wrote things like: "Can't you keep on track?" "I'm not smart enough. Why am I so stupid, dumb, and bad?" "You can't do it. You're never going to change. What makes you think it's going to be different?" and "You're kidding yourself. You're a fool."

In completing the sentence, "A self-defeating belief I hold on to about myself is . . . ," participants wrote things like: "I'm intrinsically defective." "No one is interested in what I have to say. I'm not good enough to let other people know me" and "I don't deserve a mate who is kind, generous, and loving in my life." While participants acknowledge that these statements would be cruel to speak out loud to someone else, they believe that it is the truth when applied to themselves.

Some forms of self-abuse are blatant, such as compulsive overeating, self-inflicted violence, smoking, alcoholism, or other addictions. Others are less obvious. Maybe you've attempted to pamper yourself with shopping sprees or special foods. It may only be when you find yourself overweight and in debt that you realize the consequences of your behavior. These extravagancies are sometimes self-abuse in disguise.

An upbringing that includes physical or psychological abuse often plays a role in the tendency toward these behaviors, but just as we may have learned to believe we are "no good" and therefore treated ourselves accordingly, we can learn to believe that we are capable, competent, worthwhile people. When this becomes our truth, the self-defeating behaviors will lessen.

Self-sabotage takes many forms. We can come up with a lot of creative ways to avoid change and stay in our comfort zone. Even when change is for the better and we feel motivated to change, doing so is likely to cause uncomfortable reactions. Think about how many years you've engaged in self-defeating behavior. How many years have you told yourself you're dumb, stupid, lazy, etc.? Perhaps you've heard and reinforced the idea that "you'll never amount to anything." Painful as these messages are, the more we repeat them to ourselves the more comfortable we become in believing them. We get used to them and begin to accept them as the truth.

In his tape series *Prosperity Consciousness*, Fredrik Lehrman likens our mind to an old building with long-term tenants that has been managed by the same person for years. When we decide to change, it's as if a new landlord has come in and informed everyone that it's time to change, and that the new changes are going to result in a raise in rent that will be worth the price. It's likely a good majority of the tenants are going to protest this change and say they want things to stay just the way they are. Sometimes our "tenants" are so insistent and stubborn that we give into them, but we can learn to negotiate with the parts of ourselves that resist change. Many forms of self-sabotage have an underlying theme of fear, impatience, or perfectionism attached to them. Each of these character traits can be modified with positive self-talk, goal setting, and consistent, positive action.

Who Self-Sabotages and Why?

Many individuals who engage in self-defeating behaviors describe their parents as nonsupportive, inconsistent, or rejecting. Some of us lived in homes where one or both of our parents worked outside of the home. Perhaps one of our parents was "gone" emotionally or addicted to drugs or alcohol. Situations such as these make it difficult for a child to receive the love, acceptance, and attention needed to grow and expand. Those of us who were lucky enough to escape criticism and lack of support in our homes were soon faced with the rules and regulations of society.

We spend years making our parents, teachers, friends, employers, and clergy people happy. In doing so we gradually lose touch with our true selves. We trade in our true self for the "safe" and "socially acceptable" model. Many of us fear that the potential costs of taking risks is too high to pay. We're afraid of rocking the boat, afraid to rattle our job security or make anyone mad. We rarely hear things like "follow your dreams" unless the dream is socially acceptable and financially lucrative. Money is often the central focus of career planning and we're told that money will make us happy.

According to one study, sexual abuse was correlated with self-defeating personality traits. (Vivano and Schill 1996). People in addictive, chaotic, abusive homes have not only societal pressures to contend with but the real threat of being harmed if they don't do as they are told. John Bradshaw (1989) points out that at the age of two our parents are five times our height and weight. He refers to them as "seventeen-foot, nine-inch giants" who tower over us and tell us what to do. In our childhood, we instinctively sense that we must please our parents in order to survive. After all, they are the ones who feed us, clothe us, and provide us shelter. If our parents were unstable, unpredictable, or disciplinarian, we might decide to follow along with whatever they say just to make sure we don't get hurt. As a result, we make our life decisions based on survival versus listening to our intuition and following our creative impulses.

Some of us feel additional pressure from the media. Television, magazines, movies, and songs all teach us a little bit more about what success is and it usually has something to do with purchasing a product. We are socialized day and night to reach for a standard of beauty few can attain. For those of us who were raised by unsupportive parents, this criticism might be taken personally. The bottom line in these ads is, "I'm not good enough as I am. I must change in order to become acceptable." Some of us got that message at home and in school as well.

As you read this book, you will learn how to tap into your potential, no matter what your past experiences.

What Is Success?

As you begin to move from sabotage to success, it can be helpful to understand your current beliefs about success. You may find that some of these beliefs are erroneous and self-defeating. In our culture it has become commonplace to associate success with money, awards, and achievements. There's rarely mention of happiness, being true to one's self, or even being honest and moral in most definitions of success. Success in our society is generally seen as outward attainment.

In a doctor's lobby I browsed through a copy of *Success* magazine. It was filled with tips on how to succeed in business, financial planning strategies, and advice on what to do when the stress of success gets the best of you. In that same doctor's office, I read the story of the Getty family, which was riddled with drug abuse, suicide, betrayal, and loneliness. Clearly, money, fame, and power are not necessarily the keys to a success that includes happiness, contentment, or general emotional well-being.

Many people we view as successful have self-defeating thoughts and feelings of low self-worth. *Time* magazine quotes Uma Thurman as saying, "That I'm found attractive is bizarre to me." Many stars think they are ugly and untalented and are plagued with inferiority complexes. Some of our closest friends and family members look successful on the outside, only to admit they don't feel successful and wish they could be doing something else.

This book is not about success for the sake of looking good or keeping up with the Joneses. It's about inner success. It's about following your heart, letting go of negativity that stands in your way, and allowing your innate talents and skills to shine. Sometimes as a result of acknowledging your true self you will make more money, have more friends, find the mate of your dreams, and all that other good stuff. However, when outward success becomes your primary focus, there's a tendency to move away from your true self. As a result, you will likely begin to feel disconnected, dissatisfied, and lonely. If you have a car and a home, but you also feel empty and alone, is that true success?

If your current ideas of success focus on material possessions and external achievements, you may find it useful to expand your concept of success. Rather than having external achievements and possessions be the focus of success, allow them to be the by-products of success. If you were in charge of writing a dictionary definition of success, what would you include? Is it possible that you have been trying to live up to someone else's definition of success? Writing your own definition can help empower you to live by your own standards. It's also likely that using your own definition of success will alleviate some of your feelings of failure.

Who Do You Think You Are?

As we progress through life, we tend to be placed in various categories. We assume more roles and titles. As we begin to identify with our roles in life, we may gradually lose touch with our true selves. We may become identified with our roles of parent, teacher, lawyer, and salesperson, and forget that we are also caring, compassionate, creative, and unique people. We learn from our peers and family what is appropriate, and in a desire to fit in and please others, many of us adapt our behavior. We are expected to fit into the roles society has set for us and when we don't, we're met with disappointment. This adaptation starts at such a young age that by the time we become adults, some of us are so good at "playing the game" that we don't even know we're playing it!

Raul was a lawyer for ten years before he realized he didn't like it. He was successful, wealthy, and well liked, so he couldn't figure out why he felt so empty. At the age of forty, he realized he must pursue his dream of being a musician or he'd never be happy. Prior to this epiphany he simply did what he thought was expected of him.

Gloria had a similar experience. At age fifty she realized she was trapped in roles that society had defined as female. She got married, raised a family, and kept the house, but she never felt content. She never considered the option of exploring hobbies or career interests until her kids were grown up.

People commonly ask, "What if you don't know what you want to do?" Most of us knew at some point who we are and what we wanted to do, but somewhere along the line many of us forget. In some ways it's easier to forget. There's less risk involved. If we just do what everyone else expects, no one is hurt or mad and we don't have to risk the loss of anyone's love—or so we think. What we forget to calculate is how much we hurt ourselves by not being true to ourselves. We may think that the only one we're hurting is ourselves, but it's quite probable that our inner pain will cause us to treat others poorly as well. Whether it's not being fully there for someone or hurting others with our words or actions, the inner pain caused from self-neglect can cause us to hurt ourselves and those we care about.

Regardless of how much we try to deny our true selves, they never go away completely. We can pretend to forgot who we really are, but deep down we'll always know. Even if we're in touch with our true selves, many of us are still living our lives based on that old fear that we'll be rejected if we let who we really are shine forth.

Sometimes self-sabotage emerges from a desire to keep the true self down. If you drink enough alcohol, eat enough food, or occupy your mind with enough worrisome thoughts, you can claim to be oblivious to your true self. This way you won't have to face the horrible fear of what might happen if you show others your true self. But self-defeating behaviors only put a temporary damper on your true self—you can't get rid of it completely. Nature will have its course.

So who do you think you are? Are you a punk musician, a college graduate, a corporate executive? A mother, wife, daughter, or sister? A father, husband, son, or brother? An alcoholic or an adult child of an alcoholic? A good storyteller, the life of the party, a trustworthy friend, an honest employee, or an exceptional athlete? No matter who you think you are, these categories place a restriction on who you can be. Each role you place yourself in comes with a set of rules, regulations, and restrictions. The tighter you cling to your roles the tougher it will be for you to move out of self-sabotage.

For example, Kim was the oldest of four children. She was very responsible and got a lot of praise for being so "grown up." Early on she got the idea that being silly or childish wasn't acceptable. At school she was responsible by being on time every day and thoroughly completing all her assignments. She was the first person to raise her hand when the teacher asked for volunteers and she never missed a day of class. As a teen, she felt so pressured by her responsibilities that she swung in the opposite direction and became very irresponsible. For a short time she ditched school, began sloughing off her home chores, and experimented with drugs. She developed a drug problem and began attending twelve-step groups. It didn't take long for her to become an overly responsible group member. She became a group secretary, followed the group rules, called her sponsor, and worked the steps diligently. She obtained many years of sobriety and felt it was her responsibility to refrain from sharing negative feelings that might upset newcomers. She bottled all negativity inside and even withheld the truth from therapists because she wanted to be a "good" client. Finally, the pressure was too great and she "rebelled" again.

Over the years, Kim became so attached to her responsibility role that it began to restrict her. In fact, the importance of being responsible literally drove Kim's life. It was only when she allowed herself to lighten up on her expectations that she was able to begin enjoying life. When asked to define herself, Kim said, "I'm always on time and I do what I say I'm gonna do." Many times Kim committed to projects that didn't interest her because she wanted to be responsible. Her roles and ideas of who she "should" be were determining her behavior. She was living from her mind, not her heart. Do you hold on to labels and roles that restrict you? What expectations are you trying to live up to? Who are you and what does that mean to you? Take time now to write a list of qualities that define you. Later we'll take a look at how the qualities and roles on that list might keep you stuck.

Designing Your Own Belief Tree

Our beliefs are the motivating factor behind our actions. We decide to take particular actions because we believe they will produce particular results. In a sense, our beliefs make us who we are. They determined which jobs we decided to apply for and which relationships we decided to pursue. Your beliefs have probably led you to a variety of decisions that now determine your lifestyle. A belief tree can be helpful in mapping out all your beliefs about life. On the following page, figure 1.1 shows an example of Michelle's belief tree. The highest level of boxes is for main roles you play in life. Each box below is for the rules or expectations that you've learned to associate with the role. Notice how each category we place ourselves in comes with a set of rules and expectations. Some of these rules may conflict with each other, others may conflict with our goals and dreams. When taken as law, roles can restrict our personal growth.

Michelle wrote the four major roles she plays in life. Beneath each role she wrote some of the beliefs she has internalized about those roles over the years. When you write down the expectations you have for each of your roles, jot down the first things that come to mind. The goal of this exercise is to access some of your subconscious beliefs about your roles. Don't think about your answers too long or try to come up with the "right" answer. In some cases your rules and expectations may

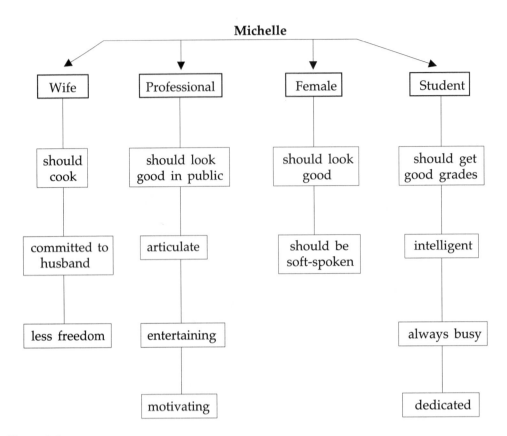

Figure 1.1

conflict with what you believe on a logical, intellectual level. However, it's usually the rules and expectations we learned in childhood that impact us most because we internalized them before we were old enough to question them, and they've shaped our deepest sense of ourselves. Even if you've worked hard to do things in a new way, try to be aware of any lingering beliefs and be honest enough with yourself to write them down.

The first thing that came to Michelle's mind for the category "wife" was "should cook." This surprised her because she actually does very little cooking. However, she said, "From the time I was a small child I have read stories, watched TV shows, heard conversations, and read ads that led me to believe a wife is supposed to cook." Under "female" she was also surprised that she put "should be soft-spoken." Michelle considers herself a feminist and supports women's rights. However, her upbringing taught her differently. She has never been soft-spoken, but says that as a young girl she always wished she could be. Her true self—the independent, free-spirited tomboy—conflicted with what her parents and society told her she should be.

Buying into a prescribed role and its rules can lead to guilt or role tension. If you're trying to be something that you're not, you'll continually have to fight against yourself. For example, if Michelle defines her roles of wife and female by rules she doesn't follow, she may feel like a failure. There are two ways to break out of limiting rules and roles: we can change the rules, and we can learn to see ourselves in broader terms—as unique individuals, not as simply a sum total of roles and rules.

Cognitive theorists say we have mental maps called schemas for every object and concept we encounter. Schemas help us make sense of the world. For example, if you're driving in the United States and see a red octagon on a sign post at the side of the road, you know long before you see the word "stop" that you are approaching a stop sign. Our schema for this object allows us to comprehend its meaning without even having to read the sign. Can you imagine how time consuming and tedious it would be if we had to read every single sign, every time we saw it, as if it were the first time we'd encountered it?

We all have schemas that help us make sense of the world. They enable us to conserve mental energy so we can use it to explore new and more complex concepts. But when we get stuck in our schemas to the point where we become rigid in our beliefs and expectations, we're headed for trouble.

For example, one of Michelle's roles is a student. Under this role she has ascribed the following rules: intelligent, dedicated, and always busy. If Michelle is rigidly attached to the role of student as her identity, she may have difficulty with free time. She may also have difficulty when she makes mistakes that lead her to feel unintelligent. If all her worth and identity as an individual is wrapped up in being intelligent, dedicated, and constantly busy, then when she is not busy or feeling especially intelligent or dedicated, she will likely suffer a momentary identity crisis. In an attempt to balance the scales and get back into her comfort zone, she might feel a need to justify herself or find something to do that makes her feel intelligent, dedicated, or busy. A healthier approach would be for her to realize that while she is a student, that is not all she is. As human beings, we'll always have days when we feel like we aren't living up to our expectations of ourselves.

In order to take charge of our lives, we need to take responsibility to examine the beliefs in our belief tree and see where they came from and whether we want to keep them. Many of us get our beliefs from sources that may not have our best interests at heart. Michelle said, "I got at least part of my belief about having to look a certain way from the media. I've seen thousands upon thousands of women in the media who look good. Because of this, I have set up an idea in my mind that females are supposed to be attractive based on these strict criteria."

Michelle decided to redefine beauty and include elements such as inner strength, intelligence, and spirituality. She decided to be more discerning when looking at advertisements and she stopped trying to meet unrealistic expectations. You may want to evaluate your own rules. Think of where they came from and ask yourself whether you want to keep them.

Changing Your Actions, Not Your True Self

In the past you may have tried to change yourself to fit into the roles you learned were important. This book is not about changing yourself to conform to the outside world. It's not about how to become more popular, how to "play the game," or how to make other people think you're successful. It isn't about how to be more socially acceptable and how to impress your friends. Instead, it's about getting in touch with your own innate talents, skills, values, and attributes, and then allowing what you already possess to guide you to success. It's about letting go of erroneous beliefs about yourself and becoming willing to embrace and accept success for yourself.

It's possible that one or more of the roles you identify with is related to your self-defeating behavior. For example, you might label yourself as "alcoholic" or "overeater" or "lazy." As you read this book, try to clear your mind of any negative ideas you might have concerning your past self-sabotage. Let go of labels you've placed on yourself and release your past mistakes.

Most of our self-defeating behaviors were developed to meet a specific need, and at one time they were effective in helping us to reach a goal. For example, if you felt the need to protect yourself as a child, you may have learned to hide your true feelings or push people away. Jacob felt powerless over his father's raging temper as a child. He turned to gambling for several years because it made him feel powerful. When he won a bet, he felt like he was on top of the world. Unfortunately, he lost more than he won and ended up feeling powerless. His family became increasingly upset with his absence and his debt increased to the point he had to sell his home. Jacob had to find new ways to empower himself that would not backfire on him in the future.

You may have developed your self-defeating behavior to cope with an intolerable, confusing, or painful event. Try to give yourself credit for being so creative and acknowledge that you were attempting to take care of yourself the best way you knew how to at that time. Now you can use that creativity and tendency toward self-care in a positive, nurturing, life-enhancing way.

Many people have feelings of low self-worth and fear that dominate their thoughts and actions. These beliefs are learned and they can be unlearned. Most of us don't sabotage ourselves in every area of our lives. This means that we already have the skills to succeed, we simply need to apply them to the areas where we need them. Just about everyone has self-defeating thoughts and engages in self-defeating behaviors to some degree. Self-sabotage results from taking self-defeating thoughts seriously. Successful people are able to put the self-defeating thoughts in perspective and make a decision not to act on them. This is something you can learn with practice.

Task List and Action Plan

Before you go on to the next chapter, take time now to do these activities. They will help you get more out of the rest of the book.

- Write your current concept of success. Where did you learn it from? Is there anything you'd like to change about it?

- Write a list of people who you think are successful. What is it about them that makes them a success?

- Write a list of people who are successful based on your expanded definition of success.

- Write a list of qualities that define you.

- Write a list of roles you play in life.

- Choose the top four roles and place them in the top four boxes of the belief tree at the end of this chapter.

- Complete the following sentence in relation to each role: "A _____ should . . . "

- Place your top four answers in the boxes below each role.

- Go over each rule and ask yourself, "Where did I learn this?"

- Put a star next to the roles and beliefs that are productive and beneficial.

- Put a check mark next to the roles and beliefs that may be creating tension or self-defeating behavior in your life.

Belief Tree

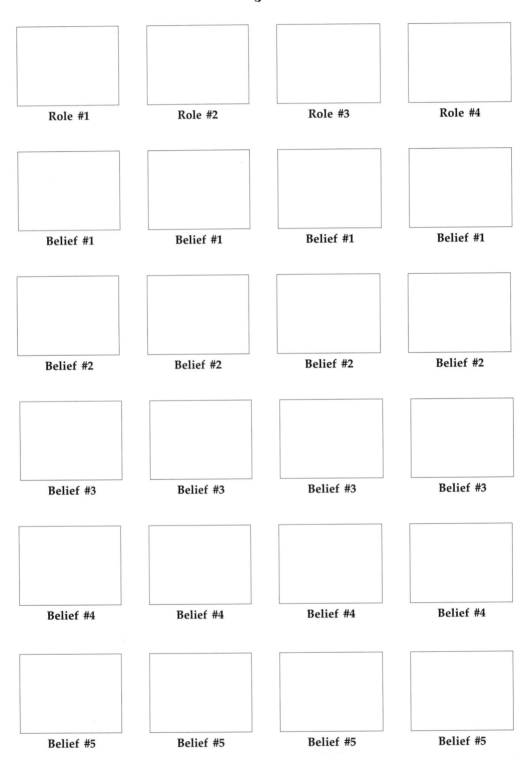

Role #1	Role #2	Role #3	Role #4
Belief #1	Belief #1	Belief #1	Belief #1
Belief #2	Belief #2	Belief #2	Belief #2
Belief #3	Belief #3	Belief #3	Belief #3
Belief #4	Belief #4	Belief #4	Belief #4
Belief #5	Belief #5	Belief #5	Belief #5

2

Self-Defeating Attitudes

This chapter can help you identify various self-defeating attitudes that stand in your way. The common forms of self-defeating attitudes have been placed in seven different categories, followed by a list of examples or points to consider. As you browse through this list, highlight or underline the self-defeating attitudes that you relate with. This will help heighten your level of awareness and begin the process toward taking responsibility for your own self-change.

Becoming familiar with the ways you self-sabotage is the first step toward stopping those behaviors. Giving serious consideration to the concepts in this chapter can help you identify some of the ways you set yourself up to fail. Many times self-defeating behaviors result from a chain of negative thoughts and potential poor choices. If you can identify the negative thoughts and poor choices as self-defeating before you engage in them, you can learn to break the chain and avoid self-defeating behaviors. You're not a victim. You make your choices, and if you don't like them, you can make different ones in the future. While identifying your self-defeating attitudes, try not to beat yourself up, or feel guilty or overwhelmed by what you discover. Think of this chapter as simply a tool to heighten your awareness.

To get the most out of this chapter, you must give serious consideration to each self-defeating attitude discussed. Watch for the tendency to minimize your self-defeating attitudes—it can become uncomfortable when you are faced with the truth of your underlying reasons for self-sabotaging. If you catch yourself saying, "Well, at least I don't ..." you could be trying to take the focus off the impact of your self-defeating behavior. You can't make permanent change unless you acknowledge your part in the problem. Upcoming chapters will show you how to change your self-defeating attitudes and behaviors, but you must identify as honestly as possible what needs to be changed in order for the upcoming chapters to be of any benefit.

Uniqueness—"I'm different. No one else is like me."

"Yes, But" Thinking

When someone tries to offer solutions to your problems, do you say, "Yes, but you don't understand, my problem is different" or "Yes, but that wouldn't work for someone like me because I have a full-time job and kids to support"? Rather than automatically saying, "Yes, but ..." why not take the information and use it to explore possibilities of what might work. Perhaps a portion of their idea will work or perhaps their idea can help you think of other avenues to explore. Take what you need and leave the rest. Don't throw out a perfectly good idea just because one little part of it won't work for you. Instead, see how you can mold and shape ideas to fit your particular life circumstances. One aspect of effective, creative brainstorming or problem solving is to explore all ideas, even the ones that seem illogical.

Comparing Yourself to Others

You'll always be able to find someone who is better or worse than you at something. Very few of us actually get to be considered the best. Even superstars are only considered the best to the majority. For example, even if you personally don't like a particular star who's popular, your dislike won't prevent him or her from becoming a superstar. Comparing ourselves to others only sets us up to be disappointed. I like the saying, "Measure yourself by your own yardstick." You may not be as successful as you want to be, but you're probably more successful than you used to be or at least much better off than you could be.

Do you compare yourself to others and always seem to measure up unfavorably? When Sheila wanted to learn how to play guitar she quickly became discouraged. She wanted to get good practically overnight, but once she got started she realized that it was harder than she expected. It required daily practice. Rather than do the hard work, she started making excuses as to why she could never be a good guitarist. She compared herself to people who had been playing since they were eight years old. She compared herself to people who had different lifestyles than her own. She would say, "If I didn't have to work all day, I could be good." It's been ten years since Sheila first got the desire to play guitar and she has made no improvement—because she gave up. If she had played guitar a little bit each day for the past ten years, she'd be quite good by now. It was only because she quit that she failed.

Making Excuses for Lack of Success

Making excuses for lack of success can lead to failure. Many times our excuses seem so valid to us that they rule our lives without question. For example, Damon wanted to get a college degree so he could obtain a high-paying job. His excuse for not doing so is that he dropped out of high school. He assumed that the college would not accept him so he didn't even try to enroll. This excuse held him back for eight years. Are you making excuses for your lack of success? Are these excuses really valid?

Having an Inferiority or Superiority Complex

Rosalie was an accomplished computer programmer. She was educated and talented. However, there was a part of her that felt unsure of herself. Whenever she started a new job she found herself in one of two situations. She either felt like everyone was smarter than her and feared being "found out," or she found herself judging and criticizing her co-workers and wondering how the "idiots" ever got their jobs. In both cases she had a hard time meeting people on the job and was left out of lunch meetings and after-hours get-togethers, cutting her out of the network that was valuable for her future progress.

If you tend to see yourself as better than everyone, or worse than everyone, you are separating yourself from humanity and saying in essence, "I am not the same." This sets you up to make excuses and avoid reaching out for help.

Perfectionism—
Things have to be perfect.

Some of us set our standards so high that we're tired before we even begin. Others start a project only to quit when they realize they aren't going to win awards. Manuel had a high school dream to become a photographer for *Surfer* magazine. He took a photography class and his first roll of film was a disaster. Everything was out of focus and some of the pictures were completely unrecognizable. He got so discouraged that he dropped the class. Had Manuel continued to pursue photography for the past twenty years, he would probably be very good at it by now. He may not have gotten a job at *Surfer* magazine, but he would have learned the value of persistence, and other opportunities may have come up. He would have also prevented the damage done to his self-esteem when he quit.

Unrealistic Expectations

Do you go into a project full-fledged, only to quit soon after? Is it possible that you are setting your sights too high, expecting yourself to do something that isn't possible or practical? It's not wrong to have long-term, lofty goals, the problem comes when you expect to accomplish a five-year goal in one year or a one-month goal in one day or one week. Slow, gradual, and steady work on a goal is more likely to lead to success than erratic spurts followed by exhaustion.

Kathleen was so eager to get into shape that she joined a gym and started taking aerobics classes. She'd previously led a sedentary lifestyle. She had no experience in aerobics. In her eagerness, she went straight to advanced aerobics. In the long run she got so burned out that she gave up the exercise program completely and didn't start again for several months.

In order to establish a lifelong habit, you need to do the same thing over and over again. It's better to start out small and work your way up than it is to start out too big and quit over and over again.

In their book, *Self-Directed Behavior*, David Watson and Ronald Tharp outline the effectiveness of setting small goals and reinforcing them with rewards. One of my favorite stories tells of a young woman with severe school phobia. She was afraid to even set foot on a college campus. When she decided to overcome her phobia, her first goal was to drive through the campus without stopping. This was followed by progressively riskier steps, such as parking the car but staying inside, then parking the car and getting out. Eventually she worked her way up to taking a college course. This process took her several months, but in the end she was successful. Had she tried to force herself to take the class without preparing herself, she probably wouldn't have even shown up the first day.

Being Too Hard on Yourself

Every life change is really a series of small steps. For example, getting a college degree begins with filling out an application and is followed by a number of steps such as signing up for classes, taking classes, taking tests, and writing papers. Failing to do one or more of these tasks would prevent you from reaching the goal of a college graduation. Yet many of us only see the end product of a diploma as a success. We fail to give ourselves credit for making phone calls, filling out forms, showing up for class, or studying. The first step to ending perfectionism is to notice each and every step you take toward change and giving yourself credit and reward for your hard work.

Having to Know All the Answers First

Having to know all the answers can cause us to procrastinate on a decision for longer than necessary. For example, Jeff wanted to learn about investing so he could plan for the future. He read many books, browsed web pages, and scoured the newspaper for information. He learned many things during his research but was afraid to put them into practice. He was afraid of the ups and downs of the market and wanted to figure out a fool-proof method for success. However, the stock market is never 100 percent predictable. Jeff didn't like that uncertainty, so he went for years without investing. Chances are, if he'd applied his knowledge and been willing to take risks, he'd have more money now than he did when he first considered investing.

Zig Ziglar, in his book, *Secrets of Closing the Sale*, uses several analogies that drive home the following point: "If you wait for all of the lights to be green before you get out of town, you'll never leave." Sometimes the only way to get the answers is to make mistakes.

Not Wanting Anyone to Know You Have a Problem

Many times, the problems that we have are obvious to everyone who knows us well and even to some people who don't really know us. Chances are, your neighbors, co-workers, and close friends and family already know that you have a problem, and they'll probably be relieved to see that you're finally doing something about it. Whatever our self-defeating attitudes are, they show up in our behavior, so most of the time we don't fool anyone except ourselves.

Have you ever had neighbors who fight constantly? Have you noticed that there are people in life who you realize you'd "better not mess with," while others will "let you get away with murder"? Each of us is sending out messages to others, and these people are making assumptions (usually quite accurate) about our confidence level, our openness to communication, and our comfort level. Chances are people treat you according to nonverbal messages you send out, whether you are aware of it or not. Sometimes we try to hide our problems from others out of shame. We deny the problem and refuse to ask for help. We think we should be able to do it on our own. This is self-defeating because, in reality, we all need help. You won't find the solution to your problems if you refuse to admit to yourself and others that you have any.

Putting On an Act

Perfectionism demands that you follow the rules, look good, do everything right, and impress others. This drive can lead you to act phony or insincere. As a result, you may have difficulties developing close, trusting relationships since you must always be on guard. Perfectionism may also demand that you have the "right" career, pastimes, and lifestyle. What is "right" by societies standards may not be right by yours. If you give in to the perfectionistic attitude that you always have to put on an act to be accepted, you may have to suppress your dreams and goals in favor of meeting the status quo.

Fortune-telling

A fortune-teller can see into the future and predict outcomes. Some of us become fortune-tellers, proclaiming we already "know" how a situation would unfold. Many of us make major choices based on our potentially faulty predictions, and some of these choices are poor and even disastrous. Paul admits he sabotaged several relationships because he "knew" how they'd turn out and took action to prevent the "inevitable" breakup. Rather than check the accuracy of his predictions or stay and improve the relationship, he packed his bags and moved on, leaving a confused mate behind.

Judgmental or Critical of Yourself and Others

Often perfectionists will be so critical and judgmental of themselves and others that they're hard to be around. Friends and family feel like they're "walking on eggshells," and that nothing they say or do is ever good enough. Lillian is so critical of herself that she's a bummer to be around. Every conversation includes a list of her downfalls. Joe not only criticizes himself but tears down everyone else, embarrassing and demeaning others. Because of this he has no close friends. Marcus can never write a report that meets his high standards, and as a result his reports are often late. This ensures that he prevents himself from succeeding.

Feeling Unqualified

George wanted a career as a journalist. He looked at the credentials of some of his mentors and noticed that all of them had master's degrees. George believed that since he did not have a degree, he could not be a journalist. He went back to school and studied hard. He was offered several internships but turned them down because he felt unqualified. He passed up opportunities to hone his skills because he was determined to get his degree first. He later realized that the hands-on experience would have been a valuable asset to his résumé.

One of the greatest ways to find out whether or not you're qualified for something is to try it. Then, when you make mistakes, you can learn from them. No amount of preparation or education will prevent you from making mistakes.

Fear—"I'm afraid to live, I'm afraid to die, I'm afraid of everything in between."

Fear is natural. The only way to make it go away is to face it. There's a saying: "Do what you fear and watch it disappear." Usually when you walk through a fear, you'll find that it isn't anywhere near as scary as you thought it would be.

Caitlin needed help preparing to talk to her ex-husband about settling their estate. She let it stew in her mind for a few weeks trying to come up with the best way to approach the topic. She ran the situation by a few people and got feedback. Finally, with sweaty palms and a pounding heart she approached her ex-husband, and with the help of a lawyer it was resolved. In fact, it was resolved so easily and quickly that she found herself on a natural high afterwards, thinking to herself with astonishment, "That was it?" Walking through that situation made it easier for Caitlin to deal with future issues regarding financial compensation.

Fear of Commitment

This fear could easily coincide with perfectionism. Many times we feel we need to make the best decision possible and then stick to it for life. This is not true. Life is about constant change and growth. We can only make the best decision possible based on our current knowledge. There are no perfect decisions, and many times we can change our decision if we find that it isn't working out.

Fear of Rejection

There's always a possibility of experiencing rejection from others, but the pain that results may be preferable to the pain of rejecting yourself to be accepted by others. Can you ever be happy living your life according to the ideas of others, or will you feel resentment and frustration at passing up the chance to be your true self? If you follow your heart, you'll attract those who support you and believe in you. Those who reject you aren't the best people to have in your life anyway.

Putting Off Your Life

Sometimes fear is so overwhelming we think we'll die. We think that if we put off doing what we fear until later, we'll somehow muster up the courage. In actuality, the only way to get rid of your fear of doing something is to go out and do it. How long have you been saying, "I'll do it later"? What's wrong with right now? Can you take one baby step toward change today? Can you make a phone call, write a letter, or clear away a few pieces of paper from the large stack you've accumulated on your desk? If you do a little bit each day, eventually you will get done what you want to. If you do nothing, you'll never see change.

Waiting for Things to Work Themselves Out

Some situations do work themselves out with time, but many times if we wait for a situation to work itself our we're subject to the whim of outside forces. Passively waiting for change to occur is a way to be victimized or disappointed. Taking an active role in working things out heightens the likelihood that it will turn out in our favor.

How long have you been waiting for your self-defeating attitudes and behaviors to work themselves out? A week, a month, a year? Twenty years, fifty years? Maybe it's time to ask for help. Many people are more than willing to help out a person in need who has a desire to change and learn.

The Pitfalls of Denial

Refusing to admit to problems is a self-defeating attitude. Since you cannot change until you admit there's a problem, denial can keep you stuck forever. Sometimes refusal to admit your problems is a result of false pride. Do you have a hard time admitting you're wrong? If so, perhaps a written inventory or feedback from a nonpartial individual such as a counselor can help you identify some areas you need to change.

If your life is falling apart around, but you pretend it's not, that's called denial. It's easy to deny the truth when you have tunnel vision and ignore the big picture. Denying things does not make them go away. One way you might identify the intensity of your problem is to write about it. Read it objectively and listen to it as if you are hearing someone else's story.

Fear of Failure

Some of us have been shamed for not being perfect. We may have experienced ridicule first hand or seen others humiliated by defeat. Somewhere along the line we may have gotten the idea that if we don't try, we can't fail. Sometimes the fear of failing stops us in our tracks before we start. It may prevent us from putting our entire effort into a situation. In any case, the fear is stifling and prevents us from living life to fullest. In actuality, the only way to fail is to quit. Everything else is a learning experience.

Fear of Expressing Your Feelings

Unexpressed feelings are like a pressure cooker—the longer you keep the lid on, the more the pressure will build up. Eventually feelings have to come out. Maybe they come out in seemingly unrelated ways, like physical illness, skin problems, obesity, stress, or inability to cope—but they do come out. In essence, you will always find some way of expressing your feelings, but bottling them up can lead to undesirable side effects. Expressing your emotions directly takes much less energy and has less compromising side effects.

Fear of Success

Some of us have learned that success is selfish. We were told not to get a "swelled head." Success can bring praise, attention, and notoriety that we might not be comfortable with. Success may place us on higher levels of leadership. Perhaps we'll be looked at as authorities or specialists. We may be expected to answer more questions or become a spokesperson for a group or organization. The expectations of others may rise once we've shown our competence. One way to avoid all of this is to stop before becoming successful. However, this avoidance comes at a price. Continued lack of success can lead to depression, feelings of failure, lethargy, and powerlessness that intrude in all areas of our life.

Needing to Be in Control

Uncertainty can cause fear. When things go the way they always have we feel safe. In our desire to avoid fear we might attempt to set up our world so that everything stays the same. Sometimes we get stuck in rigid routines that won't allow us to grow or be flexible. We might insist that others conform to our ideas of right and wrong and feel threatened when they don't. Trying to create a "safe" world is really like building our own prison. It keeps us stuck.

Focusing on Negatives—"What if things don't work out?"

Negative thinking generally makes us depressed and low in spirits. In this state of mind and body, we're less effective at everything we try. For example, if you rehearse all your past employment failures prior to a job interview, it will probably dampen your attitude and prevent you from making a good impression on your prospective employer. Rather than focusing on failure, keep track of your successes and review them often.

Lack of Motivation

Feeling unmotivated, bored, or "bummed out" can sometimes be a result of negative self-talk. Motivation comes from within and can be cultivated with daily practice. If you say, "I'm not motivated," you're saying, "I choose not to focus on the benefits of life." You can choose a new attitude by focusing on the positive aspects of change. Focus on the pros and cons of your behavior and remember, life is filled with opportunities, activities, and excitement, but it won't come knocking at your door—you have to go find it.

Excessive Worry

Worry keeps your focus on the problem and makes it difficult to find a solution. It also consumes your mental energy so you're unable to be creative and come up with alternatives. For example, Philip had major financial problems. He was in debt and had been recently laid off. He spent hours with his calculator trying to figure out how he'd ever make ends meet. He became so worried that it immobilized him. He was focused on the problem rather than the solution and felt more dismal each day. His worries made it difficult for him when he searched for new jobs. He was lacking sleep and feeling apprehensive, making it difficult for him to move forward.

Being Suspicious

Not trusting others prevents us from asking for help, reaching out, being honest, and taking risks. Sometimes suspiciousness causes us to spend extra time checking up on others or analyzing the actions or words of others. These behaviors can defeat our progress and stunt our growth. In many cases we could use this energy more productively.

Loss of Faith

Loss of faith usually leads to discouragement and the desire to quit—and quitting leads to failure. Regardless of what anyone says or does, you have the ability to maintain faith and courage. No one can take this ability away from you. At times it will be your most powerful asset. Viktor Frankl's book, *Man's Search For Meaning,* is a great example of this. Frankl was in a concentration camp, he nearly starved and froze to death, yet he kept himself alive by focusing on the possibility of seeing his wife again and speaking to the public about his life experiences and theories. Even in the midst of great tragedy, he maintained a faithful attitude. This is something all of us are capable of doing.

Unworthiness—"I'm not good enough, I'm not important."

Feelings of unworthiness lie at the root of many self-defeating behaviors. Some of us have been told we're no good by people we care about. Others of us have made a mistake we feel is unforgivable. Perhaps you've decided worthiness must be earned but you don't feel you've done anything special to earn it. Hanging on to past mistakes or feelings of unworthiness can block you from success.

Feeling Uncomfortable with Success

Some of us have mixed feelings about success. We want it, yet we feel uncomfortable when it comes our way. Some of us feel we don't deserve success. Others of us fear that if we succeed we will take good away from someone else. We may have been told that success is selfish or that depriving ourselves is a virtue. In truth, we actually help others when we succeed. We can set an example for others to follow and we can help those in need more readily. The inner sense of accomplishment and fulfillment will likely affect our attitude, making us more pleasant to be around.

Afraid to Bother Anyone

Asking for help from someone is not the same as bothering them. But sometimes we'll use this excuse as a way to stay stuck. Assuming that our requests for help are bothersome is a form of excuse-making. Take the example of two physical therapy students, Kim and Farid. Kim went to local gymnasiums and hospitals to ask about the ins and outs of the business. She interviewed people in the field and even offered to volunteer her time if she could observe her future colleagues in action. She also asked many questions in the classroom, gathering as much information as possible. Farid, on the other hand, didn't want to upset his classmates by "dominating" the class. He believed that professionals in the field had better things to do than to answer his questions. However, due to Kim's willingness to be vocal and take risks, she was assigned an internship at a local hospital while Farid remained tentative. Some people are more helpful than others, but many people like to help others. If you're asking for help from someone who seems bothered, ask someone else.

Giving Up Too Soon

Do you work toward a goal only to give up when you hit your first defeat? Do you tell yourself "It's not that important anyway," to keep yourself from feeling like a failure, even though deep in your heart you want that goal more than anything? The only way you can fail is to give up. Sometimes goals lose importance and change, but if you really want something, don't give up.

Making Yourself Low Priority

Many times we will use excuses like "It's too far to drive," or "I can't get time off work," to keep us from engaging in a self-change project. If you use excuses like this, you may want to reassess the situation to be sure you aren't making yourself low priority. For example, is it true that it's too far to drive or is it more accurate to say, "That's not a priority," or "I don't deserve it"? Do you get time off from work for birthdays, to go shopping, help a friend, or watch TV but not to work on yourself? Is it really that you can't get the time off or is it that you don't want to? Either way is fine, but there is a lot of power in the truth—when you honestly admit that you don't want to get time off, you can explore other options. Maybe you can figure out a way to achieve your goal without having to get time off work or maybe you will find a way to integrate your goal into your workday. Sometimes the reason we can't succeed is because we're busy helping everyone else but don't take the time and effort to help ourselves. We make others more important than ourselves. It's great to help others, but if all our energy is going toward others and none is going toward ourselves, eventually we'll be zapped and have nothing left to give. When we give to ourselves first, we can help others from our own fullness.

Labeling Yourself

Have you ever thought to yourself, "I'd like to do/be that, but I'm not that kind of person"? Many times the "kind of person" we are is determined by our own limited thinking. We pin labels on ourselves like "I'm not outgoing," "I'm not very smart," or "I'm not good at math." Then, because we believe this to be true about ourselves, we don't try to do anything to change it. It's true that most of us are more talented in one area than others, but it's also true that we are learning, growing, flexible, adaptive beings who can adjust to new situations. If you refuse to pin labels on yourself, you may be surprised at how talented and capable you really are.

Making Excuses for Why You Can't Change

Is it more money you need? More time? A degree? A thin body? Whatever your excuse is, letting it go is crucial to opening yourself up to change. Open your mind to new opportunities by affirming to yourself, "It is possible for me to do this right now." You don't have to believe it, just say it to yourself daily—you may be surprised at the results. Quite probably, as a result of focusing on a new thought, you'll become aware of opportunities you'd previously ignored because you were so wedded to your excuses. Many times we only pay attention to what validates our preexisting beliefs, even though there are exceptions to our ideas all around us, just waiting for us to notice.

Perhaps you've made excuses like, "I'm too old, young, fat, thin, short, tall, lazy, strong, weak, dumb, smart, poor, worthless, serious, etc." If you feel that one of the above examples applies to you, challenge yourself to begin looking for exceptions.

For example, Jessica Tandy was over eighty when she won her first Academy Award for *Fried Green Tomatoes,* and Oprah Winfrey's weight struggles not only didn't stand in her way, but perhaps made her even more famous. Autobiographies of successful people are filled with stories of struggle, abuse, and bankruptcy. It's not that successful people don't have barriers and roadblocks to success, it's that they overcome them and don't use them as excuses. Try to find at least one person who defies the generalization you use to keep yourself from trying. If you try hard enough, you will find an exception to each one. And if you don't find an exception, why not be the exception? Someone's gotta do it.

Insecurity

Behind feelings of insecurity is the belief "I can't do it." This belief can become a self-fulfilling prophecy and cause us to sabotage success and avoid risks. Risk taking is a necessary part of success. Affirmations such as "This is possible" and "I believe in myself" can help lessen insecurity. The insecure person must also take risks and walk through fears to gain self-esteem and realize their potential.

Jealousy

Jealousy is self-defeating because it relies on the belief that someone else has something we don't have. It serves to set us apart from others and keep our focus on what we don't have. Also, jealousy often includes disliking someone because they have what we want. In our minds this creates an association that "Success will make people dislike me." Since most of us desire to be loved, we wouldn't purposely do something that might bring us hate.

For example, Natasha was raised in a low-income family. She always felt jealous of classmates who came from rich families. She felt different. To ease her jealousy she told herself, "I may not be rich, but at least I'm happy." She was telling herself that being rich and being happy do not go together. When she tried to attain wealth in her adult life, she thwarted her efforts repeatedly. She found that in order to experience prosperity she had to let go of her jealous, spiteful feelings toward people with money. When she allowed herself to feel equal to people with more money than her she discovered that she could learn techniques to increase her wealth.

Defensiveness

Defensiveness can be self-defeating when we push advice and questions away because we think people are picking on us. We may refuse to examine constructive criticism because we see it as an attack rather than as potentially helpful information. Smitty made very slow progress in his business partially because anytime his friends or colleagues tried to offer him ideas, he took it as a put-down, as if they were saying he didn't know what he was doing. Smitty was unable to let go of his defensiveness and see the potential value of comments from others. Being defensive is like wearing earmuffs and blinders. You can't really hear what anyone says or see what they do. Instead you reinterpret their words to mean what you think they mean. You are on guard to prove that the other person is against you.

Self-Abasement

Some of us have committed a wrongdoing or made a mistake that we think is unforgivable. We continually hold on to the mistake and tell ourselves what bad people we are. This guilt can cause us to punish ourselves, denying our needs and wants because we don't deserve good things. We defeat our own progress by refusing to let go of past mistakes. We deny ourselves access to the opportunities of the present. You can't do anything to change the past, and punishing yourself won't make it better.

Impatience—"I want it all, and I want it now."

Impatience is probably one of the most common forms of self-sabotage. It leads to giving up too soon, doing rushed, incomplete jobs, and making snap decisions. Many people could have the successful results they desire if they'd slow down and take an objective view of their current situation. There are many forms that impatience takes and several unfortunate consequences that result. Below are just a few.

Wanting Quick Results

Sometimes in our impatience we involve ourselves in projects or plans that guarantee quick results. These decisions usually come with a pricey consequence. For example, Marion wanted to make money quickly. She figured once she made enough she could finally realize her dream of going back to school for a teaching credential. In her impatience, she fell for several "get rich quick" schemes. She spent at least a year's tuition altogether and was even further from her dream than when she started.

Not Starting Because It Will Take Too Long

Many times people decide not to go back to college or start a business because they think it will take too long. Jennifer once said to her friend, "I can't go back to college now, I'll be forty by the time I finish." Her friend's response was, "How old will you be if you don't go to college?" If you don't start today, chances are ten years down the road you'll be kicking yourself and saying, "I coulda, shoulda, woulda" done that. Why not start today and do the best you can? At least you'll have the satisfaction of knowing you tried.

Impulsivity

Sometimes impatience leads to poor performance because instead of double-checking ourselves, we do things impulsively and turn them in quickly. A few extra minutes to slow down and double check your work could make the difference between mediocre and exceptional results. Not only does rushing cause inferior work, sometimes work must be completely redone, which means you have to spend twice as much time on a project than you intended.

Feeling Rushed

Rushing not only leads to mistakes and poor performance, it can also lead to injuries and illness, which undermine a person's ability to be healthy, happy, and productive. Joseph was always in a hurry. He ran red lights, broke speed limits, and made a lot of mistakes at work. One day he ran a red light and hit another car in the intersection. He spent a month in the hospital and tapped out his savings and investments. When asked why he was in such a hurry, he admitted, "I don't know." There was no rush except the one in his own mind.

Need for Validation—"I want everyone to like me."

Sometimes in a desire to make others like us, we listen to their advice and opinions rather than listening to our own. True success, which includes contentment, peace, and joy, is based on listening to our needs. Putting others before ourselves is a way to undermine success.

Fear of Looking Foolish

People commonly avoid taking risks and exposing their true selves for risk of being made a fool of, yet your deepest, most meaningful relationships will be the ones where you dare to be yourself and the people admire you for it. Being yourself, being honest and authentic, is probably one of the best ways to find contentment and happiness. People love to be around those who are authentic—it makes them feel comfortable and free.

Fear of Stating Your Opinion

The need for validation can make it scary to state an opinion. If your opinion is different than others you may fear rejection. However, if you don't state your opinion you are at the whim of everybody else's ideas. You become a victim and may miss out on the opportunity to have your needs met. Sometimes stating your opinion will cause people to admire and respect you. Your ideas are probably better than you think they are.

Inability to Say No

One of the ways Joan sabotages herself is by spending all her time doing things for others. Joan is so busy helping others that she has no time for herself. In the attempt to gain everyone's approval, it can seem difficult to say no. You might take on too many projects or become the nurse, therapist, baby-sitter, or helper for everyone you know. Eventually you may feel taken advantage of and likely resent the very people you once adored.

Fear of Hurting Others

Sometimes people get off-track with their goals due to a fear of hurting or disappointing others. For example, Ivan was unable to admit to his parents for many years that he did not want to be a doctor. He knew this was their dream for him and didn't want to upset them. Cindy was afraid to go back to college for her nursing degree because she thought her husband would disapprove. She also felt guilty about sending the kids to daycare. Fear of hurting others can sometimes lead to lying. It can also lead to attempts to "protect" the other person.

Believing You Shouldn't Express Your Interests, Goals, and Feelings

No one can be aware of your interests, goals, or feelings unless you express them. If others are unaware they may try to please you based on what they think you want, preventing you from ever getting your true needs met. Perhaps there are people who can help you with your goals. Maybe they have an inside scoop, but they won't know to share it with you if you don't express interest.

Feeling Like You Need Approval to Make a Move

Sometimes the need for validation is so strong that we feel we cannot make a decision without approval from a friend or loved one. This places more value on the opinions of others and in essence says, "I can't make my own decisions." It gives us an excuse not to move forward, and we stay stuck.

Task List and Action Plan

Before you go on to the next chapter, take time now to do these activities. They will help you get more out of the rest of this book.

- Review the self-defeating attitudes that you underlined throughout this chapter.

- Fill out the "Top Ten Self-Defeating Attitudes, Beliefs, and Feelings" exercise that follows. Write a brief description of the self-defeating attitudes you most identify with and the consequences they have had in your life.

Summary of Self-Defeating Attitudes

1. **Uniqueness**—"I'm different. No one else is like me."
"Yes, But" Thinking
Comparing Yourself to Others
Making Excuses for Lack of Success
Having an Inferiority or Superiority Complex

2. **Perfectionism**—"Things have to be perfect."
Unrealistic Expectations
Being Too Hard on Yourself
Having to Know All the Answers First
Not Wanting Anyone to Know You Have a Problem
Putting On an Act
Fortune-telling
Judgmental or Critical of Yourself and Others
Feeling Unqualified

3. **Fear**—"I'm afraid to live, I'm afraid to die, I'm afraid of everything in between."
Fear of Commitment
Fear of Rejection
Putting Off Your Life
Waiting for Things to Work Themselves Out
The Pitfalls of Denial
Fear of Failure
Fear of Expressing Your Feelings
Fear of Success
Needing to Be in Control

4. **Focusing on Negatives**—"What if things don't work out?"
Lack of Motivation
Excessive Worry
Being Suspicious
Loss of Faith

5. **Unworthiness**—"I'm not good enough, I'm not important."
Feeling Uncomfortable with Success
Afraid to Bother Anyone
Giving Up Too Soon
Making Yourself Low Priority
Labeling Yourself
Making Excuses for Why You Can't Change
Insecurity
Jealousy
Defensiveness
Self-Abasement

6. **Impatience**—"I want it all, and I want it now."
Wanting Quick Results
Not Starting Because It Will Take Too Long
Impulsivity
Feeling Rushed

7. **Need for Validation**—"I want everyone to like me."
Fear of Looking Foolish
Fear of Stating Your Opinion
Inability to Say No
Fear of Hurting Others
Believing You Shouldn't Express Your Interests, Goals, and Feelings
Feeling Like You Need Approval to Make a Move

Your Top Ten Self-Defeating Attitudes, Beliefs, and Feelings

1. _____

How this affects your life: _____

_____

_____

_____

2. _____

How this affects your life: _____

_____

_____

_____

3. _____

How this affects your life: _____

_____

_____

_____

4. _____

How this affects your life: _____

_____

_____

_____

5. _____

How this affects your life: _____

_____

_____

_____

6. _____

How this affects your life: _____

_____

_____

_____

7. _____

How this affects your life: _____

_____

_____

_____

8. _____

How this affects your life: _____

_____

_____

_____

9. _____

How this affects your life: _____

_____

_____

_____

10. _____

How this affects your life: _____

_____

_____

_____

3

Self-Defeating Behaviors: The Result of Self-Defeating Attitudes

This chapter is designed to heighten your awareness of some of the ways you might be defeating yourself. Many times self-defeating behaviors result from a chain of negative thoughts and poor choices. If you can identify the negative thoughts and poor choices as self-defeating before you engage in them, you'll be at an advantage. This list should not be used as an excuse to beat yourself up. If you engage in one or more of these behaviors regularly, it doesn't mean that you're a failure. All it means is that you may have established some ineffective, nonproductive habits over the years. These habits can be broken. This book will help you learn to develop new habits so you can move from sabotage to success.

Procrastination

The procrastinators credo is, "I have plenty of time, it can wait until tomorrow." Sometimes procrastination stems from perfectionistic thinking. Perfectionism demands that we do it all, do it now, and do it right. Sometimes we postpone a project until we can do it all and do it right. That time may never come. When we let go of perfectionism, we can allow ourselves to break a task down into many small portions and spread it out over time. We can also allow ourselves to make mistakes, readjust, and then do things differently.

When we continually put something off until tomorrow, we may be placing ourselves in a position where our backs are up against the wall and we have to rush to get something done. In general, rush jobs aren't as thorough or fulfilling as those that are gradually improved upon with time.

If you have a project that needs to get done in two weeks, a month, or even a year, start it now. As you become more involved in the project, you can open your mind to focus on solutions and resources related to it. For example, if you're working on a term paper about the mind/body connection that's due in one month and you begin an outline, you've said to your brain, "Okay, brain, we have a term paper due in one month and we need information on the mind/body connection." Whether you realize it or not, you have just given your brain a mission. Now you will be more alert to any mention of the mind/body connection. Ideas may begin to come to you at unexpected times. In essence, you will be writing your paper as you relax and enjoy life rather than trying to cram out some ideas at the last minute.

Wasting Time

Do you diddle around with meaningless tasks while important work is waiting to be done? Are you "too busy" to do homework, clean your house, work out, go to a support group, or look for a new job—but not too busy to sit around and watch TV, sleep all day, gossip on the phone, or clean out your junk drawer? Once you recognize this as a pattern of self-defeat, you can make a decision to stop at any time.

A Sudden Desire to Do Anything
but Work toward Your Goal

Do you set aside time to work toward your goals only to break your commitment in favor of doing something less important? Does time just "slip by" without your notice? By being aware of your continual avoidance of life-improvement, you are in a position to make new choices in the future. When you feel that overwhelming urge to eat every time you try to study or make phone calls when it's time to write your novel, you can do several things. You can eat and study at the same time, or you can make a commitment to study for half an hour and then take a break for eating, picking up your studies afterwards. You no longer have to let hours, days, and weeks slip by. As you become more aware, you can allow yourself to make new choices.

Avoidance

Avoidance, not being mentally and emotionally present in the moment, and zoning out are all ways to defeat yourself. When you refuse to be mentally present, you miss out on important information. For example, Lucinda had a habit of mentally rehearsing future plans. She would miss elements of conversations and instructions from employers and college professors because she was not paying attention. This sabotaged her success in one of two ways: she did things incorrectly because she misunderstood directions, or she didn't do them at all. Because of this she missed the opportunity for high grades in school and promotions at work.

When you refuse to be emotionally present, you cut yourself off from feeling alive and experiencing intimacy with others. Bill wanted to be closer to his family, but when uncomfortable emotions arose he left the room or turned on the TV. This prevented him from gaining the closeness he desired.

Writing things down and keeping an ongoing journal can help you to identify patterns, let out emotions, and track your progress. Journaling can also help you get in touch with emotions that may be blocking you. Not writing can be a way of sabotaging your success.

Physical Illness

Getting sick doesn't automatically mean you're sabotaging yourself. However, some of us learned in kindergarten that if we told our parents we had an upset stomach they would give us lots of attention. Sometimes the only way we would get to stay home (and avoid that nasty math test or the bully who said he would beat us up if we didn't bring him our lunch money) was if we were sick. Ask yourself whether there is consistency or a pattern to your illness. If you repeatedly get sick prior to important events and then use it as an excuse not to participate, physical illness may be a form of self-sabotage.

Physical illness as a form of resistance is difficult to acknowledge because many of us do indeed get sick and we have the physical symptoms to prove it. The mind is very powerful. Self-talk can in some cases create illness and produce cures. If you get sick every time you have a job interview or every time you have finals in school, then maybe it's time to take a look at whether or not you're sabotaging yourself with physical illness. I've known students who've admitted to getting sick right before class and then being "miraculously" cured once class was over. It seems that they manifested feelings of illness as a way to avoid class, especially since they recovered once the stressful event was over.

Changing the Subject

When someone says something that makes Tim uncomfortable, he pretends he didn't hear them. He changes the subject so he doesn't have to deal with the uncomfortable feelings that come from facing it directly. Changing a subject doesn't change situations and events—it simply postpones them and allows them to build up.

Leaving the Room

This is similar to changing the subject. Something happens that makes us uncomfortable, and rather than openly communicating, we leave the room. Changing rooms doesn't make a problem disappear, it simply postpones it and possibly allows it to grow bigger.

When Debbie first started attending twelve-step meetings, she was very uncomfortable and afraid of change. Every time the break came she went to the bathroom (whether or not she really needed to relieve herself) in order to avoid getting close to anyone who might talk her into changing. If you have conditioned yourself to associate uncomfortable situations with escaping to another room, you can unlearn that behavior and put a new one in its place.

Looking Away

Do you avoid your feelings or fears by refusing to look people in the eye when they talk to you? Do you dart your eyes around the room when something important is being said? Avoiding others is a way to miss out on important information. Next time you find yourself avoiding someone, try to remain focused and open—you never know what you might be missing.

Avoiding Emotional Intimacy

Being close to others offers a variety of benefits. When we share our thoughts and feelings with a trustworthy individual it can help us to realize we're not alone. It may help us feel better about our situation when we see that most people have fears similar to ours. Friends and family can be a source of support, helping us navigate rough times and stay on track with our goals. Isolation or keeping to ourselves can make problems seem larger than they are. Keeping our goals to ourselves may make it easier for us to put them off because we believe that this way no one will know if we don't follow through. Finding supportive people can help us to move forward quicker than we would by ourselves.

Indirect Communication

Communicating indirectly has several consequences. If you don't clarify yourself, you may not be understood. Perhaps someone will act on what they think you mean and you will be disappointed, thinking it's someone else's fault. For example, Clarita was always mad at Philip because when she said, "This kitchen is a mess," she expected him to know her true meaning, which was, "I want help." Philip felt nagged and Clarita felt overwhelmed. Had Clarita directly and lovingly asked for help, she probably would have gotten it. Instead, this couple got trapped in a cycle of misunderstanding that nearly destroyed their relationship.

When Grace and Herman met up at a class reunion, Grace happily walked toward Herman, glad to see him. Herman was cold and distant, and Grace was confused. Evidently, Grace had hurt Herman's feelings the last time they saw each other five years before, but Grace was unaware of this. Only hours later would Herman finally admit what was on his mind. By then the reunion was over. Herman's indirectness caused him to hold a grudge for five years and spoil what could have been a wonderful event for both himself and Grace.

Feeling Distracted

Distraction is a great way to avoid learning, growing, and changing. Susie was always doing something distracting during her conversations. Whether it was putting on lipstick, flipping her hair, or playing with her earrings, she was never 100 percent involved in a conversation. Many times people were offended by her seeming lack of concern. Sometimes she missed her bosses' instructions because she was busy playing with her computer or flipping through her Rolodex. It wasn't uncommon for people to become extremely irritated with her because they took her distraction as an indication that she didn't care about what they were saying.

Compulsions

Compulsive behavior takes enormous energy to maintain. It's emotionally consuming. While engaging in compulsions we have myopic focus, keeping us from seeing the big picture. All our focus is on feeding the urge within. Whether we abuse food, drugs, alcohol, or shopping, or we feel compelled to engage in other self-defeating behaviors, our lives lack balance in the midst of compulsive behavior. When all our energy is directed at compulsive behavior, we lack objectivity and may cut ourselves off from new activities and opportunities that would promote our personal development.

Sometimes our compulsions add a new set of problems that also become time and energy consuming. For example, overeating could lead to excess weight, compulsive shopping could lead to excess debt, and substance abuse can lead to legal and financial troubles. These issues consume even more of our time and energy, leaving us depleted and unable to focus on achieving new goals.

Overeating

Many people overeat to stuff down feelings or punish themselves. Some feel nurtured when they overeat but experience a sense of failure over weight gain. If you have a compulsion to overeat, thoughts of food and eating may become overwhelming, making it difficult to focus on anything else. In many cases overeating takes us away from our true self. It consumes energy that could be used to attain goals and better our lives.

Drug Abuse

Drug abuse has some of the same consequences as overeating, but it also places us in the position of doing something illegal. Many men and women are spending time in jail, separated from loved ones and wasting money and time battling with the courts. All this time and energy is likely to deplete a person's resources and leave little or no time for self-improvement.

Alcohol Abuse

Alcohol abuse is legal, but deadly nonetheless. It leads to embarrassment, as well as marital, legal, and health problems. Even "controlled" alcoholics have the burden of covering their tracks, lying to loved ones and worrying about being found out.

Shopping

For some people, shopping can become compulsive. If you spend time shopping at the expense of taking care of your daily responsibilities, you could be a compulsive shopper. Do you spend endless hours looking for good deals, watching the shopping channel, flipping through catalogs, or driving long distances to take advantage of sales? Is your life out of balance? Do you shop in lieu of working on self-improvement? Shopping can also lead to overspending and excessive debt, which will be covered later in this chapter.

Self-Defeating Habits

Self-defeating habits often make a situation more difficult than it needs to be. These time-consuming habits sap our energy. The time and energy required to maintain these habits could be used to help us reach our goals and move toward the life we desire. These habits are based on choices we make. They have nothing to do with outside influences, which means they can be changed. We can learn new, self-enhancing habits if we are willing to put in the time and energy to do so.

Lying

Dishonesty almost always has a cost. If we lie to cover something up or impress someone, we place a tremendous pressure on ourselves to perpetuate the lie. If our lying is discovered, we risk losing things we value.

Smoking

Smoking kills. It's known to cause lung cancer, emphysema, and birth defects. Smokers are increasingly being separated from nonsmokers in public places. In some cases smoking is used to deal with emotions or avoid feelings. It's a time-consuming habit. Many smokers postpone their work because they have to wait and finish their cigarette. The average smoker smokes one pack per day. If each cigarette takes five to ten minutes to smoke, the smoker spends over two hours a day smoking. With cigarette prices on the rise, smoking is also costly. This is money and time that isn't being used constructively.

Being Disorganized

Being disorganized can cause us to lose important papers, miss deadlines, or forget important appointments, meaning we have to spend a lot of time and money relocating or repurchasing items we've lost. Being disorganized takes a lot of extra time and energy that could otherwise be used toward achieving our goals.

Being Late

Being late is one way to sabotage your success. It can cause stress and can upset friends, relatives, employers, and clients.

Timothy was a realtor. He was frequently late when he met with clients to show them new homes. Some clients became irate and left before he showed up. Others refused to do business with him again. Lawrence was frequently late in other areas of his life as well. Several of his friends decided they could no longer tolerate his tardiness. They felt disrespected and taken advantage of when they rearranged their schedules to be with him and he didn't show on time.

Irresponsibility

Irresponsibility can lead to a variety of unfortunate and energy-consuming consequences. Generally, lack of responsibility has a way of catching up with us sooner or later. Whether it's missed opportunities, late fees and fines, or having to make up for past mistakes, irresponsibility can cause us to waste a lot of time and energy. It can also cause us to feel overwhelmed and scattered. It may deplete our creative energy, making it difficult for us to break free from our self-defeating cycle.

Risky Behavior

Do you put yourself in situations that make it difficult or impossible to attain your goal? For instance, a newly sober recovering alcoholic probably shouldn't hang out in a bar; a person who recently quit smoking should probably stay away from situations that tempt or trigger the old feelings and behaviors. This doesn't mean you have to live in a cave, just be realistic. It takes time to get used to new changes and to build strength.

Missing Important Meetings and Appointments

If you're a member of any ongoing support or networking group, you'll get the greatest benefit when you attend regularly. This way people get to know you, you get to know them, and a sense of trust and harmony builds. Missing meetings means missing out on valuable information and distancing yourself from the members whose support and guidance you may need someday.

Missing appointments is also a way to sabotage your success. Why do you miss the appointments? Do you say it's because you forget? If so, begin a new reminder system—call and leave yourself telephone messages, leave reminder notes in obvoius places, or program your computer to remind you of things. Write appointments down or ask your friends to give you a reminder call. In this day of advanced technology, there are many ways to remind yourself of your obligations. Take charge of the situation and do what you can to change it.

Not Making Important Phone Calls

If you tend to avoid making important calls, try doing something to remind and motivate yourself. Try giving yourself a reward for each call made. You can also try making the less threatening phone calls first. Once you're warmed up to being on the phone it will likely be easier to make the more difficult calls.

Not Writing Things Down

When something is in writing it's a permanent record that can be referred back to when needed. Some people sabotage themselves by neglecting to write things down. If you consistently forget appointments or misplace important information, you may want to consider keeping written records that you can refer back to when needed. For example, keep all important phone numbers in one central location. Write down information you may be likely to forget such as dates, times, and driving directions. This way you have a backup if your memory fails you. Sometimes the act of writing something down heightens the likelihood of future recall. It can also save you time and energy in the long run when you don't have to gather the same information over and over again.

Excess Debt

Many of us live beyond our means. This is often a result of impatience and need for validation (wanting to keep up with our peers). Credit cards have become a too-easy backup for emergencies and other times when we have no money to spend. Debt is costly. If you don't have enough money to begin with, debt can drive you further into a hole.

Continuing to go into debt can get you locked into your current job and lifestyle, preventing you from feeling able to make changes toward success.

Forgetfulness

Sometimes our fears become so overpowering that we forget important things. It's as if the fear freezes our brain and we become overwhelmed or confused. Fear is often precipitated by a series of negative or catastrophic thoughts about life. These thoughts can be changed with daily practice, helping the intensity of fear to lessen.

Overspending

Overspending places you in a position of stress and struggle. If you spend more than you make or live paycheck to paycheck, you'll be overwhelmed and consumed when an unexpected (yet normal) expense comes your way. Car repairs, illness, accidents, birthday parties, baby showers, and many other events are a part of life. If you're prepared for them, these kind of expenses don't have to be a major ordeal.

Codependent Behavior

According to Codependents Anonymous, codependency is a set of behaviors we adopt to gain a sense of control and security in our lives. It stems from a need for love and approval and can lead to denial of self, low self-esteem, compliant behavior, and controlling behavior. Codependent behavior can include putting others first or valuing the opinions of others over your own. Below are some self-defeating behaviors that can result from codependency.

Remaining in Harmful Situations

Some of us remain loyal to a person or institution even though it has been harmful or self-destructive in our lives. For example, Lynne stayed with her job for ten years out of guilt and fear. Her boss was verbally abusive and overly demanding, but Lynne was his only employee and she felt her boss needed her and would be lost without her. She negated her wants and needs in favor of remaining loyal to her boss. Joe stayed married to a verbally abusive woman for thirty years because he was afraid she'd "fall apart" without him.

Going Along with What Others Want

Being overly compliant and doing what everyone else wants is a way to delay your own progress. When you're overly compliant, you spend time and energy doing what everyone else wants rather than exploring your own wants and needs. Susie spent three years in college going along with the crowd. She took classes that her friends took, went to parties, and never took time to think of her own goals. Now, five years later, she's frustrated with her lack of progress and wishes she could be further along in her education.

Listening to People Who Say You Don't Need to Change

People in your life may want you to stay the same because when you change it's uncomfortable for them. Remember that you're changing for yourself and you are important. Other people will come and go, but you will always have to look at yourself in the mirror. Being true to yourself will probably have a positive effect on your relationships. Sometimes it will bring an end to limiting relationships, which are often replaced with harmonious ones. Sometimes your self-change will motivate and inspire change in others.

Asking for Help from the Wrong Person

Sometimes we pretend that we're willing to change, though deep down we're so scared that we really aren't willing to change at all. We do a lot of work, but not the work that will most effectively help us reach our goals. We ask for help, but not from qualified people who have the answers we need. This way, we can say, "It's not my fault, I keep trying," and not really accept responsibility for our lack of progress. When you ask for help, are you asking qualified people? When you do work on yourself, are you doing work that will help you reach your goals, or is it just busy work that makes you look like you're working hard?

One example of asking for help from the wrong person is when we seek advice from a negative, perfectionistic person. Juanita continually asked her cousin for help on a writing project before submitting it. Her cousin never thought Juanita's work

4

Awareness Is the First Step toward Change

Unless you acknowledge and identify your self-defeating attitudes and behavior, you cannot change. In the previous chapter, you identified the ways you sabotage yourself—which means you're already on the road to success. Once you realize that you are the one resisting change and standing in your own way, you can do something about it. Once we stop thinking it's someone or something "out there" causing our problems, we can stop feeling stuck and powerless.

One of the things that keeps a lot of people stuck is needing to know all the reasons behind self-sabotage. Understanding your reasons for self-sabotage is not necessary in order for you to make changes in your self-defeating behavior. This book is action-oriented—you can use it now. You don't have to analyze your past and figure out why you got this way, all you need is willingness to change. This book teaches skills. It will focus on new ways of doing things. If you practice the new and change the old, your life will change accordingly. This can begin to happen whether you delve into your past or not.

Heightening Your Awareness to Ensure Greater Success

In order to begin self-change, you'll need to become aware of many things. First of all, ask yourself, "What do I want to change, and why?" If you don't have a clear idea of what it is you want to change, you'll never know whether or not you're making progress in the right direction. It's very important, yet sometimes difficult, to isolate exactly what you want to change and what your life will look like once you've made that change. For example, if you want to lose weight, don't just say "I want to lose weight." Be specific. How much weight do you want to lose and what do you want your life to be like as a result? Do you want health, happiness, thinness, security, and confidence? Then write that. State your goal clearly—"I want to lose thirty pounds, and I want to feel confident and secure in my body."

Then ask yourself why you want to make this change. Is it for yourself, because you want a better life, or do you want to change because your partner, child, doctor, or employer told you that you should? If you're trying to change solely because other people want you to, you may lack the motivation to follow through. Most of the time, in order for permanent change to occur, you must want it for yourself. However, there are ways to motivate yourself if you truly think that changing is in your best interests.

For example, if you have a problem with procrastination and it's leading to problems with your employment or relationships, you may need to change your ways even if procrastination doesn't bother you or seem like much of a problem. It can help make change easier if you focus on the positive aspects of change. If you begin planning and working ahead of schedule, you will probably do a more thorough job and have less stress. Projects may get done while they are still manageable rather than turning into monumental tasks. Focusing on what's positive about change can help you when you are tempted to go back to old ways.

If you have a big project to complete, you may want to put it off one more day. If you're tempted to procrastinate, first take a mini inventory of the pros and cons of doing so. Here's how it might look:

Pros	Cons
get to relax	feel more pressure tomorrow
get to watch my favorite show	might not get project done right or on time
	might lose my job or the respect of my boss
	might embarrass myself

Writing a pros/cons list can help you discern whether or not you're ready to change. All change entails positive and negative payoffs. Take a look at both sides. Are the positive payoffs for changing more powerful than the negative ones? Will you gain more than you'll lose by embarking on this project? Is there sufficient reason to change? How do you want your life to look five, ten, fifteen, or twenty years from now? If you want your life to be different tomorrow, you have to change what you do today.

Once you've determined that you're willing and ready to change, you can increase your awareness of some of your roadblocks by using a structured method of journaling (see exercise at the end of this chapter). Keeping a structured journal will help you to identify some of the patterns that lead up to your self-defeating behavior. The first step in structured journaling is to identify your goal. What behavior do you want to change and why? Be as specific as possible and limit yourself to one thing for right now. If you want to work on changing other behaviors later, you may do so, but for now start with the most important thing you want to change so you can learn the techniques and build your confidence.

One of the ways we sabotage ourselves is by taking on too much at once. We have unrealistic expectations and are let down when we find out we are not superhuman. There is no need to change everything right now—you have plenty of time to make all of the changes you want. When deciding what behavior you want to change and why, you may want to take into consideration the consequences of this behavior. What happens when you engage in this self-defeating behavior? How does it feel? How does it affect your family, your physical and emotional health, and your employment? You'll also want to consider what benefits will be gained by attaining your goal. All behavior has negative and positive consequences. Sometimes the consequences of our self-defeating behavior seem solely negative, though they may hold positive value to us anyway. They serve as distractions or keep us comfortable because they are familiar. For example, the negative consequence of sabotaging relationships is that you never get to form a lasting, meaningful bond with anyone. However, there is safety in staying distant, so if safety is important to you or you fear intimacy, the consequence may be experienced as more positive than negative. Before you set your first goal, take into consideration where you are now and try not to set a goal that is too far from your reach.

Antecedents

Now that you've identified your goal, take a week or two and keep track of the thoughts, feelings, and behaviors that you engage in that either support or undermine your progress. For example, James wanted to start a freelance carpentry business and eventually quit his job as a grocery clerk. His excuse for not doing so was that he had no time. His assignment was to keep a daily log of what he did each day so he could decide which activities to cut down on and how he could maximize his time so he could use it more wisely. He was also asked to keep track of his excuses. For example, James had no obligations on the weekend, yet he always came up with excuses for not doing woodwork. Once James was able to see his schedule on paper, he realized he was making invalid excuses for not moving forward. He was able to come up with a schedule for himself that would include about ten hours each week to work on carpentry.

He continued to keep a written schedule, keeping track of what he actually did during the ten hours he was supposed to be doing woodwork. Sometimes James did his work as planned and he felt great. Other times he let excuses get in the way. He wrote down his excuses and went over them with a trusted friend. He found that most of his excuses were related to perfectionism. He told himself, "I don't have enough time to finish this project now, so I'll do it later." James was convinced that if he didn't have time to do the whole thing, he shouldn't do it at all. He was encouraged to break his projects down into manageable steps and give himself credit for each step. He began focusing on progress rather than perfection. Gradually he began finishing projects and selling them. Along the way he learned efficient use of his time.

Having a clear record of why you don't follow through on your desired behavior should help provide you with clues as to potential obstacles to making permanent change.

Stress and negative self-talk are major antecedents to a lot of unwanted behaviors. Let's say you wanted to change careers, so you begin looking for a job, searching for information about different companies, updating your resume, and going on interviews. Then, you suddenly lose steam, get tired, feel defeated, and give up. Keeping a journal can help you to see what led up to your feelings of defeat. It could be that you were thinking negative thoughts like, "I'll never get a job in this economy" or "Nobody is hiring now. I'm just wasting my time." It could be that you put so much pressure on yourself to get a job that you are stressed out and therefore less efficient and self-assured. Stress can create a frantic, busy, insecure state that is not conducive to life change. The good news is that the stress and negative self-talk can be eliminated. You're not flawed or helpless, you've just been dealing with the situation ineffectively—and you can change that.

Breaking the Old Routine

Once you've had a chance to see the chain of events that leads up to self-sabotage, you can place new links in the chain that make it less likely for you to act out in old ways. Sometimes your environment is a major cause of unwanted behavior. Many studies have shown that crowded, drab environments create stress and depression. Rearranging the furniture or going outside for a change can often lead to a change in behavior. Sometimes we can assign moods and behaviors to an environment. If you always eat in the dining room, sitting there might remind you of eating. There may be cues in your environment that continually trigger old responses. For example, the beer ad you see every day on your drive home may be prompting you to want a drink. You may have overeaten after work so many times that every time you walk in the door after a long day at work, you think about eating. Sometimes we form habits that become so ingrained that we don't even realize we're engaging in negative behavior until it's too late. See if you can break this chain by adding a new step somewhere in between or doing things in a different order. Maybe instead of walking in the door, heading for the refrigerator, and grabbing a beer or some food, you can take a hot bath, go on a walk, or work in the garden. Then, once you've relieved some stress, you can decide whether or not you still want a beer or food.

Try driving home from work a new way, walking to the store instead of driving, taking a few deep breaths on the way to the mailbox, reading in the backyard instead of the living room, changing the order of your morning routine—anything to interject new behaviors into your current routine.

Take pauses before automatically engaging in old behaviors. If you're tempted to engage in your self-defeating behaviors, write about it first. Outline your feelings and explore the consequences of the behavior you're about to engage in. Take a few deep breaths or say some affirmations. Tell yourself, "I will overeat in five minutes if I still feel like it, but for now I am taking a time-out." These things may seem simple and unrelated to your goals, but you never know where your behavior originates from and breaking a link in the normal chain of events may lead to a different end result. Rearranging your schedule or taking a two-minute pause before engaging in old behavior can help you to break out of your comfort zone physically and put a wrench in the wheel of automatic behavior.

Sometimes we use our self-sabotaging behaviors as our "reward" for a hard day's work. We feel that we "deserve" to treat ourselves after all the work we've done. But many times these rewards aren't very fulfilling. We may like the alcohol and food while we are ingesting it, but once we stop, we still feel pretty miserable. We may feel "too tired" to pay our bills or go grocery shopping, so we zone out in front of the TV instead—only to panic at the end of the evening that we haven't even made a dent in our responsibilities. Why not replace these habits with something that truly is a reward to you. Take a moment now to list things you enjoy doing and see how you can integrate them into your daily life. You do deserve rewards for your hard work, just make sure that your rewards are things that make you feel good about yourself and not just pacifiers to make up for an unfulfilled life.

After you've journaled and identified some of the thoughts and feelings that lead up to your undesired behavior, take some time to write about the behavior itself. Even if you do something counterproductive to your goal, take a moment to write about what happened during the day and how you feel about your relapse. Try to find cues that will show you the chain of events that led to your self-defeating behavior so you can put a stop to things next time *before* they get out of control. What did you do exactly? Did you lay on the couch and feel bad about not exercising? Did you eat a box of cookies? Did you yell at your partner? Did you hang out with your friends instead of doing your homework? Write out what happened and also write what time of day it happened. For example, you might write something like: "I wanted to exercise, but I came home from work and was so tired that I just sprawled out on the couch. I told myself that I'd get up and exercise in fifteen minutes, but next thing I knew, I fell asleep and when I woke up it was already 6:00 and I had to cook dinner." After writing about the behavior itself, write about how you felt as a result of engaging in self-sabotage.

If you overate, how did you feel? Lethargic? Unattractive? Depressed? Energized? If you yelled at your partner, what was the outcome? Did you get what you wanted? Did you feel guilty? Did you kiss and make up? If you fell asleep on the couch, what happened and how did you feel? Again, sometimes our consequences are both negative and positive. Sometimes the chaos in our lives creates a smokescreen that allows us to ignore other bigger problems, and that's much more comfortable than trying to change. Sometimes we feel comfortable with our negative behaviors and their consequences because they are familiar to us. The goal is to engage in behavior that is most effective in producing desired results in our lives and let go of behaviors that aren't getting us to where we want to be. Using structured journaling can teach us a lot about ourselves and our relationships with others. Writing things down helps us to break out of the denial and rationalization that seems more powerful when it's just in our minds. When it's on paper it can be seen more clearly and then reevaluated and changed.

Breaking the Cycle

Just because you have a pattern of sabotaging yourself doesn't mean you have to continue this pattern. With heightened awareness and a willingness to change, you can stop yourself at any time before or during the act of sabotage and do things differently. One night Janie, a recovering overeater, drove into the parking lot of an ice cream eatery because she wanted to use her coupon for a free scoop of ice cream. As she drove in the lot she paused and asked herself, "Am I really hungry for this or am I coming here simply because I have a coupon?" Once she realized that she was not hungry for the ice cream, she pulled out of the parking lot and went on her way.

Just because she'd pulled in the parking lot didn't mean she had to walk in the store. She had a choice up to the very last minute. Even if Janie had gotten out of the car and walked in the store, she always had the choice of walking back out. Even if she got the cone and started eating it, didn't mean she had to finish it. And, even if she had eaten it, she still had the choice as to whether or not she would feel guilty.

Most of the time sabotage is not irreparable—you can turn a situation around by acting quickly and honestly. If you are in the middle of doing something that is not for your highest good, stop immediately and do something differently. It's not too late. If you've already done something you regret, you have a choice as to how you view it. You can be hard on yourself, living in guilt, anxiety, and fear, or you can let it go and learn from it so that next time you will be able to make a better choice. As long as you hang on to the past, it continues to control your decisions, keeping you from moving forward and making positive changes. No matter what you've done, it's over. Now, see what you can do to make sure it won't happen again.

Let's say you're a procrastinator or you have a habit of wasting time. Maybe you're the kind of person who decides to clean out the sock drawer five minutes before it's time to leave for an important job interview. Perhaps you decide to alphabetize your CD collection when you are in the midst of finals and have four papers to write in one week. Maybe you sabotage your relationships by becoming cold and distant or starting fights. Maybe you've had an affair or engage in other self-destructive behavior within your closest relationships. When you heighten your awareness of the various ways you sabotage yourself, you can begin making choices. You can choose to put those socks away, messy or not, and stop yourself in the middle of alphabetizing your CDs, deciding to come back to them after finals are over. You choose your behavior. You're not a victim. It may not be easy to change, but it is possible.

Stages of Awareness

Many of us become most aware of self-sabotage as we look back and reflect on the projects, goals, or relationships that didn't work out the way we planned. We may notice after a breakup of our second or third significant relationship that we are repeating the same pattern over and over with different people. We may become aware of our own self-defeating behavior when we hear ourselves complain about our job to a friend for the fiftieth time. This level of awareness is what I call stage one awareness, and it's an important precursor to change. With honesty, open-mindedness, and willingness, you can learn to heighten your level of awareness and identify sabotaging behaviors *before* you engage in them, or at least before you do irreversible damage.

Josephine wanted to improve her parenting skills. She wanted to stop yelling at her kids and become more patient. When she saw Tony headed for the house with muddy sneakers her first impulse was to yell, "Tony, you'd better not walk on my clean floor with those dirty sneakers! How many times have I told you about that?" Instead, she paused, took a deep breath and walked out to meet Tony. She put her hand on his shoulder and gently led him to the hose. She said, "How about if we rinse your sneakers off over here so you don't track mud in the house?" Josephine realized that just because she felt like yelling didn't mean she had to follow through.

There are three basic stages of awareness:

1. Being aware of something after you've already done it

2. Being aware of something while you're doing it

3. Being aware of something before you do it

With time and patience, you can learn to heighten your awareness so you don't have to keep repeating the same mistakes. Mistakes are part of the learning process. By using the tools in this book, you can learn how to grow from old mistakes and move forward.

The Importance of Self-Care

Sometimes a major reason for our lack of motivation and inability to succeed can be as simple as poor self-care. Stress, lack of sleep, and poor nutrition are all things that will stand in the way of success. In twelve-step programs, they advise their members never to become too hungry, angry, lonely, or tired, as these states of being increase our likelihood of indulging in negative behaviors. Usually these states create stress, and stress leads to negative thinking and a lower level of self-esteem, which is an enemy to us when we desire positive self-change.

Victor had a goal to become less judgmental and critical of himself and others. He kept a judgment journal for a few weeks, writing down his judgmental thoughts, who they were directed at, and the circumstances surrounding them. At the beginning of the project he described himself as someone who "couldn't stop judging people all the time." However, through journaling, he noticed that he was really only judgmental of certain people under certain conditions. There were some people he never judged. Also, there were times and places when his judgment flared up more than others, like when he was tired, rushed, or hungry.

Keeping a journal helped Victor realize that he wasn't a mean person, he simply lacked skills in certain areas. He could learn to change his behaviors with practice. By getting proper rest, eating right, and managing his time wisely, Victor was able to cut down on judging himself and other people.

Perhaps some of your attempts at self-change have failed simply because you were too tired, trying to do the impossible. All of us have a natural body rhythm called a circadian rhythm, which determines when we're alert and when we're sleepy. Some of us are more effective in the morning and some of us are more effective at night. Paying attention to your own body's rhythm and working with it will also enhance your chances at success.

You might want to keep a journal of your energy levels for a week or two. See if you notice any patterns in regards to your mood or effectiveness. Try to take care of important tasks in your "peak" hours and avoid serious conversations during your low times. Nobody is "on" twenty-four hours a day. Being aware of your alert times will help you decide the best way to organize your life.

There are several tried and true ways to reduce stress that don't take much practice, including deep breathing, exercising, and meditation. Using these techniques can help you avoid extreme stress, which makes it more difficult to resist self-defeating thoughts and behaviors.

Deep Breathing

Deep breathing is an easy, effective form of stress reduction. Try setting aside about five to ten minutes each day to do nothing but focus on your breathing. You can do this in a sitting or standing position. Simply stop all activities and take in several long, slow, deep breaths. Feel your lungs expand completely, then exhale slowly. Imagine that you are breathing in and out of a straw and only a small amount of air can come in and leave at a time. Feel the rhythm of your breath and allow your body to slow down. Chances are, you will feel an almost immediate sense of calmness and relaxation.

When you are calm, your mind is more effective. You're in a place of power. You're not subject to acting on impulse. You're in a position to view your situation rationally. For greater effectiveness, try this deep breathing exercise several times throughout the day. Make it a habit so that if you encounter stress, you can use deep breathing to help you relax and handle it more calmly. If you think you don't have time to do this, take into consideration that if you take time for deep breathing, you actually save time in the long run. Rather than spinning in circles or making costly, time-consuming mistakes, you'll be in a position to do things right the first time.

Exercise

Exercise is another proven method of stress reduction. There is a plethora of information available about proper nutrition and exercise techniques. All people, regardless of their weight or age, can benefit from exercising at least three times a week and eating a balanced diet. I'm not going to recommend specific exercise or eating plans here. I recommend instead that you discuss the matter with your doctor and find a health plan that's right for you. What's important is that you find something you enjoy and do it consistently. Start where you are in your fitness level and increase from there. If you're not accustomed to exercising, start small. If you decide to use walking as your form of exercise, start by taking short walks. Then, as you feel comfortable, increase the length of your walks and the pace of your step until you are walking briskly for at least twenty minutes, three times a week.

As you begin to feel more comfortable with your exercise routine, you may want to add variation by combining cycling, walking, aerobics, yoga, swimming—whatever appeals to you. It's very important that you don't try to force your body to do something that it isn't comfortable with. Chances are this will just cause you to give up and feel like a failure.

Your diet can have a tremendous effect on your stress level. Foods with high sugar, fat, and caffeine content tend to fatigue the body and make it function less effectively. If you decide to modify your diet, remember to be patient with yourself and cut things out of your diet one at a time. Find a way of eating that you'll be able to stick with for the rest of your life (of course, you'll probably make adjustments as time goes on). Remember, one of the forms of self-sabotage is perfectionism, so don't try to be perfect overnight. Start where you are and improve from there. Once you see the benefits of proper nutrition and exercise, you'll be likely to continue with little or no effort.

Meditation

Meditation is an excellent way to relax and take time out for a new perspective on life. Take about five to fifteen minutes a day, preferably in the morning, to close your eyes, breathe deeply, and concentrate on the silence, on your breath, on the beating of your heart. Allow your mind to drift and be free from any obsessive planning. Focus on the moment. During this time, you may also want to ask for guidance from your higher self as to what steps you need to take to move in the direction of success. As you become more aware of your inner guidance, follow it and allow yourself to effortlessly let go of unwanted habits and behavior. There is a part of you that knows what to do. Meditation is a time for focusing on the wise part of you that is always there.

There are many forms of meditation and many philosophies on the best way to meditate. You may want to delve into these various methods later. In the meantime, you'll experience meditation's benefits if you simply set aside quiet time and allow your worrisome, troubled thoughts to drift away. You may decide to do this with your eyes closed or open. You may find one thing most helpful, be it a bubble bath, a swim in the pool, or simply doing what you normally do but paying attention to the moment—really being 100 percent present, not worrying about the past or the future, just being aware and open to your surroundings. You may find that just by doing this you become aware of things you haven't noticed before, you remember things you've forgotten, you get inspired to call someone you haven't spoken to recently.

Meditation places you in a position to be open to your surroundings. It gives you a space to think before you act or react. These benefits sometimes solve problems in and of themselves without your having to use techniques, lists, plans, and goals. Meditation can also help you to become more aware of your true self, from which you may have been hiding. When you pay attention to this true self, you're more likely to succeed.

Task List and Action Plan

Before you go on to the next chapter, take time now to do these activities. They will help you get more out of the rest of the book.

- Assess your level of awareness (1, 2, or 3) as outlined in the beginning of the chapter.

- How can you work toward better eating, sleeping, and exercise habits? Choose one goal and act on it today.

- Are you a morning person or a night person? Are you attempting a difficult task at a non-peak time? If so, how can you change this situation?

- List one or more stress reduction techniques that you can begin doing every day this week.

- Identify the specific areas you want to change. Then choose one and write it on the awareness worksheet. Then complete the rest of the worksheet.

- Make an effort to become aware of the ways you sabotage your success. Write down any insights you have throughout the week and see if you can identify ways to overcome or anticipate future self-sabotage.

Awareness Worksheet

1. What do you want to change and why? (be specific) _____

_____

_____

_____

2. What do you need to do to accomplish this change? _____

_____

_____

_____

3. What's holding you back (real or imagined)? (list self-defeating behaviors and attitudes that you've identified) _____

_____

_____

_____

Do you really want to change? Or are you doing it for someone else? (circle one)

What are the pros and cons of changing?

Pros	Cons

List some of the times you've been successful.

1. _____

2. _____

3. _____

4. _____

5. _____

On a scale of 1–10, what is your level of willingness to change? _____

Sometimes we engage in self-defeating behaviors because we feel unfulfilled in our lives. List at least ten things that you like to do and put a check mark next to one of them, signifying your commitment to follow through on doing it this week.

1. _____

2. _____

3. _____

4. _____

5. _____

6. _____

7. _____

8. _____

9. _____

10. _____

Date:

Structured Journaling

Behavior I want to change (be specific): _____

_____

What I want to replace this behavior with (be specific): _____

_____

How I plan to do it (first step): _____

_____

1. After a week, answer the following questions in your journal:

When I tried to work on my new behavior, this is what happened: _____

_____

_____

2. What I did (positive or negative): _____

_____

_____

3. What I felt like afterwards: _____

_____

_____

Sentence Completion

Another tool to help you develop awareness of the things that stand in your way is sentence completion. Here are some examples taken from Nathaniel Branden's book, *Six Pillars of Self-Esteem* (1995), and Shakti Gawain's book, *Creative Visualization* (1978). Put an ending on the following sentences and see what comes up for you:

1. At the thought of becoming more successful _____

_____

_____

2. One of the ways I obstruct my progress is _____

_____

_____

3. If I can allow myself to be successful today _____

_____

_____

4. The reason I can't have what I want is _____

_____

_____

5. The reason I cannot break out of myself and become more of who I want to be is

_____

_____

6. I learned this from _____

_____

_____

   Your answers can give you a better idea of what may be standing in the way of your success. Here are some examples of sentence completion's that were written by my workshop participants.

> *The reason I cannot break out of myself and become more of who I want to be is that I have never been successful, so at this age I don't think I can. I am trying, but I'm only fooling myself. I can do things for free but am not smart enough to make money. I believe this because I haven't gotten anywhere in my present job.*

> *The reason I cannot break out of myself and become more of who I want to be is that I have a feeling of never quite belonging, never quite fitting in. I feel like most of the time I have to be "on." Only in a few circumstances do I feel I can relax and be accepted for being me. I learned this from childhood. I was a foster child. I never felt like I was good enough to be a real part of the family. Also, I grew up being told, "A child should be seen and not heard." Seems the only time I was happy was when I was married and had a family. But then my spouse left me for someone else after fifteen years. More rejection.*

> *The reason I cannot break out of myself and become more of who I want to be is my fears of rejection and of making a mistake. I never feel like I'm capable. Also, I'm a perfectionist. I have unrealistic expectations. Changing my behavior will take too much of my time. I will miss out on something else. I believe this because whenever I do my best, someone else always seems to be able to do it better than I can. I won't measure up to what others expect of me. My parents always said, "Who do you think you are?" whenever I tried to succeed.*

Do you identify with any of these statements? In the upcoming chapters, we will be looking at how to change these negative, self-defeating beliefs into positive, life-affirming ones.

5

What You Say Is What You Get

Often we sabotage ourselves because fear gets the best of us. We fear success, we fear failure. We fear love and we fear rejection. Fear stems from our thought process. We think: "If I succeed, everyone will be jealous," or "People will try to take it all away," or "If I fail, I'll never be able to show my face again." We think: "If I really let myself love this person, they will devastate me," or "If I call that person, they may not be receptive to me and it will hurt my feelings." Self-sabotage occurs when these thoughts dictate our actions. We "think it through" and decide not to make that phone call, not to open our hearts, not to write that book, not to pursue our dream career. Our thoughts affect our behavior and ultimately determine our success or failure.

Fortunately, you can change your thoughts. You have control over what you decide to think, focus on, and perceive. To make changes in your thinking and eventually in your self-defeating behavior, you can use repetition of new, positive, and life-enhancing thoughts. You can create and use positive self-statements to change your thinking and create new behaviors. Positive affirmations help open your mind to new possibilities. They gear up your mind to accept new ways of thinking, making it easier to change. Noticing your resistance to affirmations can teach you about reasons you sabotage yourself. Once you are aware of the beliefs that need to be changed, you can create specific affirmations to target your areas of concern and make the progress you desire. The following table offers examples of how our self-talk affects behavior.

How Self-Talk Affects Behavior		
Original Thought	**Action**	**Result**
"I'll never lose weight."	I might as well eat this cake. What is the point of going to the gym?	Your thought comes true. You don't lose weight. You were "right."
"No one ever helps me."	So I might as well do it myself (and not even give them the chance). I won't even bother asking for help.	No one helps you. They learn from watching you that you like to do everything yourself. They feel powerless or useless around you because you never let them do anything.
"I have a hard time meeting new people."	Act fearful, defensive, or shy around new people.	Others view you as standoffish or rude and are hesitant to get close to you.

"All men are creeps, they only want sex."	Focus on all examples that validate this truth. Take all compliments about your looks as a come-on. Ignore all men who are not trying to pick up on you. Give in to sexual advances easily.	You don't allow yourself to meet a man who sees you as a whole person. View all nice men as boring and fake.
"Women are nags and only want a man for his money."	Take suggestions and comments as criticisms. Don't ask questions, merely assume you know what the other person means. Look for examples to support your hypothesis. Watch TV shows that portray this type of woman because they are the ones that are "realistic" and that you can "relate" to.	Cold, distant, defensive relationship of inequality. Hurt feelings, loneliness, disappointment. Fear, never feeling good enough, rebellion.
"Young people these days have no respect for elders."	Put all behaviors in this context. Refuse to remember yourself as a child. Refuse to take actions to gain respect because "there's nothing you can do."	Distance from young people; they don't want to be around you because they never feel good enough. You don't respect them so they don't respect you. Vicious cycle. Everyone wants to be right.
"In today's society, people only look out for themselves."	So I'm gonna look out for myself.	Loving, trustworthy people are put off by your selfishness, so you never meet them.

Of course, not all of our beliefs are negative. Some might be positive such as, "I'm a good cook" or "I'm a fast learner." However, whether positive or negative, they have the potential to be limiting. For example, if you identify yourself as a fast learner, you are likely to take pride in that quality. However, if a situation comes up where you are unable to learn a new concept or task quickly, you may feel like a failure or inadequate. You may want to give up. The ideal is to be flexible enough to accept that there are exceptions to the rule. When your mind is fixed on a limited number of beliefs, it's not open to the totality of possibilities. When you place your focus on trying to prove your beliefs right, you can't explore alternatives.

In order to make changes in your life, you'll have to challenge some of your beliefs. There are many factors that shape your concept of reality, such as the neighborhood you grew up in; your socioeconomic status; the era you grew up in; influences from your parents, teachers, friends, and the media; your gender; your religion; or your race. Based on your limited life experience, you form generalizations about what life is all about. No matter how old you are, how far you've traveled, or how high your education is, you have yet to experience everything in life, therefore, your thinking is limited.

Affirmations are a tool to help create an opening in your mind. Once a small opening has been created, it makes way for an abundance of ideas, beliefs, and creative thoughts to come forward. When you plant new ideas in your mind on a daily basis, your perceptions will begin to change. You will see the world in a new way. Your mind, in its desire to be right, will search for evidence to support your new-found beliefs, and you will likely find it. If you keep an open mind, you'll be amazed at the opportunities and realizations that present themselves to you. Sometimes you will become aware of opportunities and ideas that have been around for several years, yet because of your old way of looking at the world, you blocked them from your consciousness.

Beliefs Create Reality

Beliefs sometimes act as blinders, causing us to ignore what doesn't support our thinking and notice only what fits into our schema of life. For some of us, our beliefs make up our identity. For example, if you're a male who believes that a good man provides for his family and shows no emotion, you may have made career success and emotional denial a part of your identity. The more firmly you hold on to beliefs for your sense of identity, the more you will refuse to see anything that negates or challenges your thinking. An example of extreme thinking might be found in someone with anorexia. Persons with anorexia believe themselves to be fat, and therefore that is what they see. When they look in the mirror, they block out all information that negates this idea. Even if they wear a baggy size one or only weigh eighty pounds, they will still proclaim that they are fat, and that is truly what they see.

Interesting research has shown time and again that our perceptions of ourselves affect our behavior. In the film *A Class Divided*, Jane Elliot demonstrates a lesson plan she created to teach her first grade students why discrimination was wrong. She divided the class into two categories, students with blue eyes and students with brown eyes. For the next two days, each group took turns wearing a special felt collar. The group who wore the felt collar was discriminated against for one day. They were not allowed to drink out of the water fountain and could not play on the playground with other children. They were chosen last for group activities and given less attention in the classroom. It did not take long to notice a difference between the two groups where there had been none prior to the experiment. The group with the felt collars were slower and had more behavior problems. The group without the felt collars appeared smarter and were better behaved. When the experiment ended, the teacher discussed it with the children. They all reported hating to wear the felt collar and said they felt stupid when they wore them and smart when they didn't. They also reported feeling superior to the group who wore felt collars. This experiment shows not only the effects of discrimination, but also how our self-concept affects our behavior.

An interesting study was done with elementary students and their teachers. Researchers told teachers that a certain number of students in their class were "late bloomers" and were expected to make great academic gains. In truth, all students were identical in academic potential. Eight months after the teachers were told about the "gifted" students, researchers came back to the classroom to find that, indeed, these students were doing better than others in their class. It seemed that the teachers had a positive outlook for these students and therefore spent more time with them. The positive treatment affected the students, allowing them to improve their grades (Rosenthal and Jacobson 1968).

Perhaps you've bought into negative expectations from others. Maybe you've taught others to have low expectations of you. Negative self-talk can often work in a circle. You think you're not good enough, so you associate with people who support your belief. They set expectations and limitations on you and you live up to them. Marietta recently realized that she taught her children by her words and deeds that she can't do anything. Her children now chime back their teachings and tell her, "You can't do it," anytime she embarks on a new project. We are continually teaching people how to treat us. Others can read our nonverbal cues such as, "You don't really have to do what I say because I'll pick up the slack," "You don't have to be on time because I'm never ready for you anyway," "My ultimatums don't mean a thing, I never follow through on what I say I'm gonna do. My threats are empty," or, "I don't feel comfortable talking about feelings and showing affection." If you don't believe in yourself, how can you expect others to do so? You may have had unsupportive family members who said you were no good, awkward, or untalented. With the use of affirmations you can take away the power of these negative statements.

There is a saying, "It's easier to believe a lie you've heard a thousand times than it is to believe a truth you've heard only once." A lot of times what we believe to be the "truth" is really a lie we've decided to believe. Because we believe this lie so strongly, we create a world that supports it so we can stay comfortable. Most people prefer to be right. One way to make this happen is to go through life finding evidence to support our beliefs, negating any evidence to the contrary.

Change Your Perception

Using positive self-talk helps change your perception. No matter what happens in life, you have the opportunity to view it in an empowering way. If someone breaks up with you, you can choose to think about how they hurt you, how they did you wrong, how you'll never trust anyone again, or you can focus on how great it is to be single and how much you learned from your ex-mate and how wonderful it is to be out of a relationship that isn't right for you.

All life experiences offer opportunity for growth. There is always a different perspective to be taken and focusing on various perspectives can help change your attitude, resulting in greater peace and happiness. Changing your perception is not about lying to yourself, it's about choosing to see the big picture and looking at a situation from all angles so you can be empowered versus feeling helpless. Filmmakers and scriptwriters know that the camera angle affects the impact of a scene. In a script you will see the letters: POV, standing for "point of view." The same scene shot from different angles has a different psychological effect on the viewer.

If you are in a classroom with thirty people, some of you will be in the back, some in the front. You will each be sitting next to different people and you will have a different view of the speaker than other members of the audience. All of this tends to affect your perspective of the event.

As a form of empowerment, why not choose to open your mind to various perspectives? For example, if a person says something to you that you perceive as hurtful, you can view the situation in a variety of ways. You could think:

1. That person is out to get me

2. Maybe they don't mean it the way I took it

3. Maybe they are projecting their issues onto me and this really has nothing to do with me, or

4. Maybe they were talking to someone else. Taking a moment to view other perspectives gives you the opportunity not to act on impulse. This is not possible if only one viewpoint is taken into consideration.

Affirmations: A Tool to Change Beliefs

Affirmations or positive self-statements are a simple tool you can use to help change your belief system. Affirmations are simple, but they aren't necessarily easy. Using affirmations can be difficult because it requires you to change some of your ideas about life that you have nurtured and held on to for many years. Because you're challenging old beliefs, you'll probably feel uncomfortable with this process, especially in the beginning. It's natural to experience resistance when starting this process, and at times it may feel like your mind is fighting against you. This change in beliefs can stir up a lot of emotion and cause you to wonder if it's worth all of the effort. Rest assured that the resistance and fighting will pass, at least until you decide to move on to changing tougher, more deeply rooted beliefs.

A positive affirmation is a statement made in the present tense that represents what you desire to bring into your life. Use these statements in place of negative self-talk, and as your self-talk becomes more positive, so will your attitude and expectations. Say these new statements to yourself as if you believe they are the truth. A teacher of mine once told me that affirmations are the truth told in advance. There are many forms of affirmations, and I will cover some basic points to help you formulate effective affirmations. Once you learn about affirmations and how to formulate them, you'll then need to use repetition to get them stuck in your mind so that eventually you replace the negative, self-defeating thoughts that you now hold with positive, life-affirming beliefs. The reason you accept your beliefs as truth is because you've heard them over and over, for many years. Affirmations require a lot of repetition before they become a natural part of your thinking.

Affirmations for Self-Improvement

The following pages will outline affirmations you can use to improve different areas of your life. Many times people become frustrated when trying to develop their own affirmations. The examples provided can help get you started. Use this list as a guide. Once you get comfortable you can learn to write your own affirmations. In the meantime, feel free to reword or combine any of the following affirmations to suit your needs.

Affirmations are more effective if you focus on one area of self-change at a time. If you gather a list of ten affirmations on different topics, you'll be scattering your energy. Try focusing on one or two areas of self-change at a time. Once you experience success in an area, you can rearrange your affirmation list to reflect your new goals. Remember, one of the ways to sabotage yourself is to have unrealistic expectations. Be patient with yourself. Be willing to go slow and get the most out of these affirmations.

As you work with affirmations you are likely to experience resistance. Use resistance as a learning opportunity. Affirmations are likely to activate defensiveness and stir up the deeper beliefs that have been holding you back. For example, Joseph wanted to clean out his garage and let go of some clutter. Each time he tried the project he became overwhelmed and gave up. He always found something better to do. When he started to write affirmations about becoming clutter-free and achieving his goals, his thoughts were, "You'll never accomplish this. You don't make wise decisions. You always throw the wrong things away then regret it later. You've never been good at finishing things." Joseph realized that these thoughts were deeply rooted within him and they made it difficult for him to accomplish anything or make firm decisions. Rather than focus on affirmations about the garage, he began to focus on self-love, self-forgiveness, and trust. He found that this helped him not only with the garage but many areas of life.

This chapter contains affirmations for a variety of situations. You can either read the section that interests you or read the entire thing. As you go through the lists of affirmations, make note of those that resonate with you. Later you will be instructed on how to institute these affirmations into your daily life so they can become true.

The following affirmations address some of the common issues that contribute to self-sabotage. Remember, an affirmation is a positive self-statement that's often the opposite of statements you usually say to yourself. Affirmations are designed to challenge your automatic responses and help you change your perspective.

Overcoming Sabotage and Resistance

- Growing and changing is exciting, even if I have to look at some painful things inside me in order to do it.

- All my changes are easy to make.

- When one door closes, another door opens.

- I am willing to drop old benefits when they no longer work for me.

- I am willing to honestly look at the way I do things and say, "I don't want to do that anymore."

- I am willing to change.

- I am free from limitations of the past.

- I am free to go forward.

- I am willing to release my resistance to change.

- I am willing to release the need to be unworthy.

- I am worthy of the very best in life and I now lovingly allow myself to accept it.

- As I build my feelings of self-worth, I no longer feel a need to push away good things.

- I am willing to release the pattern within me that is causing me to self-sabotage.

- The more I learn to love myself, the easier it is to refrain from self-destructive behavior.

- I am triumphant over negative, self-defeating thoughts.

- I am ready to have the life of my dreams.

- I am constantly growing, changing, and becoming a better person.

- I see myself as a winner who succeeds at everything.

- I am capable of change.

- I have and will continue to be capable of taking steps to improve my life.

- I release the old and make way for the new.

- I am grateful for all change and growth in my life.

Improving Self-Esteem

- I am willing to experience a higher level of self-esteem. I deserve it and I am ready for it.

- I am a unique individual and a creative being.

- I am enough right now.

- We are all worthy and deserving of high levels of self-esteem.

- The more I develop my inner sense of self-esteem the better I feel about my body, my job, my relationship, and all other aspects of my life.

- I take time each day to focus on what is good about me.

- I am smart, talented, and capable.

- I celebrate my uniqueness.

- It's okay that I'm not like everybody else—that's what makes me special.

- I take time each week to do something that pleases me, even if it seems frivolous.

- I treat myself the way I would treat a good friend.

- I take time to get to know myself and I treat myself with respect.

- I listen to myself because I am valuable.

- I do something each day to improve my self-esteem.

- I am beautiful inside and out.

- I am lovable.

- I like myself for what is in my heart, not for the way I do things.

- I accept myself as I am.

- I am a powerful and loving person, and I count.

- I feel precious even when I know that I have made a mistake.

- I am alive, I am here, and I am worthy.

- I am beautiful, strong, and energetic.

- I believe in me, I believe in what I think.

- I see myself as the person I want to be.

- I am interesting, I am valuable.

Body Image and Weight Loss

- I am willing to be nice to my body and to do what is best for it. I deserve it and I am ready for it.

- I give thanks for my eyes, nose, mouth, and ears. I am grateful for the fullness they have added to my life.

- I treat my body with respect.

- My body is miraculous.

- My body is smart.

- I trust my body.

- I cancel out negative thoughts about my body.

- I think positive thoughts and encourage my body to be the best that it can be.

- I keep a mental picture of my desired body in the forefront of my mind.

- I believe that I can have the body I choose.

- Because I love my body, I give it optimal treatment and allow it to become as healthy and vibrant as possible.

- The more I love myself and others, the easier it is for me to lose weight.

- I love my body enough to allow it to become thinner and healthier.

- I walk, talk, eat, breathe, and act like a person who has a healthy, attractive body.

- I maintain the right to decide what is attractive by my own standards.

- I like the way my body feels.

- My body has a lot to tell me and I am willing to listen.

- I love and accept my body right now.

- My body is a miracle, no one else is exactly like me.

- Because I love my body, I only do what's best for it.

- Everything I do creates a better body for me.

- I am excited about the changes that are taking place in my body right now.

- I am beautiful, sexy, energetic, and healthy.

- I decide what goes in my mouth and how much I exercise, therefore, I can and will become fitter and healthier.

- My habits are evolving and I am becoming the toned, healthy person I want to be.

- I prefer my body to have a light, healthy feeling over a heavy feeling.

- I am willing to do what it takes to become healthier.

- I am ready to have the body of my dreams.

- I love and appreciate my body, my mind, and my feelings.

Relationships

- I am willing to engage in healthy relationships.

- I treat my friends and relatives with respect.

- I deserve love right now.

- I release old hurts and dare to live in the now.

- I am now attracting healthy, loving relationships into my life.
- I dare to make the first move and communicate my feelings.
- I feel confident and comfortable with others.
- I dare to tell the truth.
- Love flows freely through me.
- I give and receive love freely.
- I allow myself to experience the benefits of a loving, supportive friendship.
- I release the past and allow love to heal every area of my life.
- I accept the love and wisdom my friends and relatives have to offer me.
- When I live in the now, I can see my partner as perfect, whole, and complete.
- I'm still me in any relationship.
- The right person is out there, I am willing to be patient.
- Feelings of love come from within. I can feel loving and loved regardless of the people in my life.
- I work on myself, and I'm becoming the kind of person who would make an ideal mate.
- I communicate openly and honestly with my partner.
- Open communication is invigorating and freeing.
- I look at my mate through the eyes of today and I see his or her beauty like never before.

Sexuality

- It is safe for me to feel sexual energy.
- I let go of fears regarding expression of my sexuality. I express my sexuality in healthy ways.
- I decide what creates sexual feelings for me, how I want to be sexual, and with whom.
- I let sexual energy work for me in creative ways.
- I affirm my sexuality beyond gender, roles, and expectations.
- My body belongs to me.
- I accept and affirm my sexuality today.
- I celebrate my sexuality.
- I allow my sexuality to emerge.

Health and Fitness

- I am willing to be a healthy person.
- I am experiencing exuberant health.
- My body is a miraculous gift.
- My body deserves to be treated with respect.
- I deserve the good feelings that come with taking care of my body.
- I feel healthy and I love myself.
- I am creating a healthy body.
- I enjoy nutritious foods.
- I select only those foods my body requires for proper nutrition and optimal health.
- I develop a stronger health consciousness every day in every way.
- I am healthy. I eat properly and I exercise regularly.
- I exercise for health. I am health conscious.
- I enjoy exercising daily. I see myself as I want to be.
- I create positive habits in order to improve my health and move toward wholeness.
- I clear all emotional blocks and negative energy from my body. As a result, it functions beautifully.
- I love to exercise and eat well. I love to be energetic and happy.
- I let go of all burdens, I clear all blocks, I allow love to flow through me and heal all ailments.

Peace and Happiness

- I love to receive compliments and I compliment myself and others often.
- I feel so good about myself that I want to share with others.
- I tell at least one person each day that they are beautiful and special.
- I am happy to replace depression and lethargy with energy and enthusiasm.
- I release heavy, burdensome thoughts and feelings. I release anger and resentment.
- I express my emotions appropriately.
- I am grateful for the life experiences that have brought me to this point.

- Peace, love, and living life wholly are mine today.

- Feelings just are and they will pass.

- I accept all life experiences as they are now.

- I know that everything happens for a reason and I look with joyous expectation for the lessons each experience is trying to teach me.

- I go with the flow. I do what is in front of me and all else falls into place easily and effortlessly.

- I take time daily to list all the things in my life I have to be grateful for. I have a great life.

- I focus 100 percent of my attention on the task at hand and therefore experience life with a sense of wonder and contentment.

- I would rather be happy than right.

- I look for and find happiness in my daily routine.

- I am open to happiness.

- Happiness comes from within.

Prosperity

- My every thought leads to opulent living.

- I attract beauty, joy, and abundance into my life.

- I attract good things.

- Abundance equals flow. As I put energy into my work, it comes back to me in the form of money.

- My money is a mirror of the abundance I believe I'm meant to have. I respect it, enjoy it, and act responsibly with it.

- I am prosperous. I refuse to entertain thoughts of lack.

- Living prosperously sets an example for others to follow.

- I am opulent in the abundance of life.

- Every moment of my life is an enriching experience.

- I see abundance everywhere.

- The seeds of prosperity planted in my mind are plenteous and flourishing.

- I am affluent.

- Living prosperously means living fully. It means acknowledging and accepting the love and abundance that life has to offer. There is nothing selfish about it.

- Living prosperously means that life is working with me and I am working with life.

- Prosperity comes to me in many ways. Unexpected income is one of them.

- My income is expanding and increasing right now as I read this affirmation.

- I'm on the road to financial success.

- I am open to and aware of all forms of prosperity, including but not limited to gifts, income, and ideas.

- Living prosperously means having the audacity to live my dreams.

- I have plenty to spare and plenty to share.

- When one person prospers, we all prosper.

General/Motivational

- I feel empowered and in control.

- My life is a wondrous creation.

- My mind has unlimited potential.

- I vividly imagine myself as I want to be.

- I am confident in my ability to succeed.

- My mind is open to new ideas that help me get things done.

- When something needs to be done, I do it.

- I am a doer. I get things done.

- I am an achiever.

- I am successful because I get things done.

- I do things now, I do what I need to do.

- My mind is my greatest asset. It helps me get things done.

- I have an alert mind and calm body because I do things now.

- I can make my dreams become reality.

- I believe that change is possible for me.

- I am greater than the assumptions I have about myself.

- I clearly see that nothing and no one can stand between me and my own good.

Spiritual

The following affirmations are designed to heighten spiritual awareness. Many contain the word "God"; however, you can replace "God" with any alternate words you use to describe your focus of spirituality.

- I am a precious child of God.
- I am willing to surrender and trust my Higher Power.
- My Higher Power and I can handle it.
- Whoever touches me touches a precious child of the universe.
- The light and love of God are now working in and through me.
- I am willing to follow the guidance from my Higher Power to the best of my ability.
- Whatever I am doing, God is with me.
- Everything happens for my highest good.
- I live one day at a time with God's help.
- With God, nothing is impossible.
- For this moment, I choose to let go and let the universe lead me to my highest good.
- I take time to feel my spirit, to stay in touch with who I really am.
- Today I will cultivate and listen to my higher self.
- I allow my Higher Power to enter my life today and cherish the serenity that follows.
- I will step aside and let God take over.
- Today I dare to radiate a spirit of love, joy, and happiness.
- I trust the universe to bring about the perfect fulfillment of good.
- Today I will listen to my inner voice and be guided in the right direction.
- Today I initiate change and place the outcome in God's hands.
- God's will is better than anything I could imagine.
- There is nothing but God.
- The infinite mind is my true resource.
- I am unlimited because the universe is unlimited.

Assertiveness/Boundaries

- I am still me in any relationship.

- I have the right to set my own boundaries.
- I take action to set my boundaries and improve my self-esteem in all relationships.
- It's okay to change my mind.
- Today I am learning to be comfortable with my own power.
- I am willing and able to speak for myself.
- I respect my own needs for personal safety and set boundaries to achieve it.
- It is safe to say no.
- I mean what I say and I say what I mean.
- I deserve to be heard.
- I ask clearly for what I want and need then wait to receive what's best for me.
- I set and keep standards that are deserving of my positive worth.
- I can take all the time I need before answering a request or a question.
- I am smart, talented, and capable.
- I attract loving, supportive, trustworthy people into my life.
- I am manifesting a high level of self-confidence.

Dealing with Uncomfortable Feelings

- I am creating safe ways to express anger.
- I am vulnerable when it is safe.
- As I allow myself to grieve, I heal my sadness and create space for love.
- I can allow myself to be cherished and supported in healthy ways.
- I feel whole and alive while experiencing my feelings.
- I move through anger to find the sources of my hurt and fear when I need to do so.
- I do some of my deepest, most potent growing in the soft moments of my life.
- In my vulnerability I discover newfound dimensions of strength.
- I will use my anger as an energy source to fuel the course of action I know I must take.
- The moments when I feel pain teach me more about who I am and what I need.

- I will survive my pain and take courage from overcoming it.

- My feelings are temporary and fluid.

- I express myself in an effortless and carefree manner.

- All feelings are acceptable.

- I let go of the past, I let go of the future. Life is too short to waste valuable time dwelling on things I cannot change.

- I can change this moment, this moment is anything I want it to be.

- Challenges promote growth.

- I accept and experience all of my feelings.

Career

- I take time to listen to the needs of others.

- I am open to new ideas and opportunities.

- Each day I take steps that lead me toward my goals.

- I am a good listener.

- I am successful at whatever I do.

- I work in an atmosphere that nurtures me.

- My gifts are welcomed and appreciated.

- I am surrounded by talented, interesting, motivating co-workers.

- My work matters, and I feel fulfilled.

- Each person I work with, be they co-workers, colleagues, or clients, is blessed by my giving.

- My work makes a positive difference in the world.

- My business thrives.

- I am open to ideas that would increase my business.

- I look around at the people who are doing the kind of work I would like to do and making the kind of money I would like to make and I dare to ask them how I could go about doing the same thing.

- I am taking the necessary steps toward doing the work that feeds my soul and stuffs my pocketbook.

- I keep my eyes and ears open.

- Ideas, opportunities, and resources surround me.

Goals

- I set goals—short-range goals, long-range goals, goals that enhance my life and the lives of others.

- I plan my work, I work my plan.

- My goals are specific and achievable.

- I prioritize my goals.

- I optimize my energy because I am goal oriented.

- I review my priorities regularly.

- I visualize my goals.

- I write down my goals.

- I realistically look at what needs to get done and set reasonable priorities.

- I stretch, without straining, for more of life and the positive energy it holds.

- I focus attention on what I want to accomplish and it all gets done easily, effortlessly, and on time.

- Today I take steps toward attaining my goals.

- I take care of business today.

- I am motivated to pursue my goals.

- I fulfill my potential as the day unfolds.

- I have the resources to meet whatever life brings.

- I have within all I need to achieve my dreams and desires, all I need to do is step out of the way.

- I am willing to _____ (fill in blank with action you need to take to attain your goal) because I desire the transformation of my life.

Stress

- I am in control.

- I confront difficult situations in a relaxed, confident manner.

- Breathing deeply and slowly helps me to relax.

- When I feel pressure, I relax the tension in my muscles.

- I have an alert mind and calm body.

- I function effectively under pressure.

- When I feel pressure, I focus on my breathing.

- I feel stress-free today and live in joyous existence.

- I take a deep breath and assess the situation before doing something I will regret.

- Today I would rather be happy than right.

- I am willing to experience peace, joy, and harmony.

- I let go of the past and the future.

- In this moment, everything is exactly as it should be.

- As I take time to relax, my mind provides me with solutions to my problems that are creative and ingenious, and that work for the good of myself and others.

- I take time to meditate or exercise when I feel stressed, knowing that when I do, I come back more efficient and effective than ever before.

Fear

- I triumph in the face of adversity.

- I have the courage to change.

- I have the courage to feel my fears.

- I can dare to take a risk.

- My courage enables me to overcome challenges and turn obstacles into stepping-stones.

- My faith lifts me above my fears.

- I do what I fear and watch it disappear.

- I let go of worry, fear, and doubt. I choose courage, faith, and peace.

- I allow my fear to transform into excitement, enthusiasm, and anticipation.

Impatience/Unrealistic Expectations/Perfectionism

- I continue working toward my goals as long as it takes.

- I have wonderful goals and the dedication and persistence to make them come true.

- I have faith that my dreams will manifest themselves in the right time and in the right way.

- I am patient and persistent.

- I am going through changes at the perfect pace for me.

- Each moment is an opportunity to create a new and improved me.

- Today I relax, let things happen, and just enjoy myself.

- I let go of unrealistic expectations. I am willing to be part of the process. I take one step at a time. I applaud my progress.

- I do the best I can and release the results to the universe.

- I am perfect, life is perfect, everything is working out as it should today.

- I am willing to be humble.

- I am willing to ask for help.

- I start where I am and do what I can.

- I give myself credit for every baby step I take toward achieving my goals. Every step is important and valuable.

- I give myself permission to make mistakes.

- I notice changes in my life and I like them. I feel great.

- I am perfect in all my imperfections.

- I see the best in everything.

- Today I avoid crisis by refraining from overdoing, overorganizing, and overscheduling.

- Today I focus on my triumphs, not my tragedies.

Taking Risks

- I have the audacity to try new things today.

- I welcome change with joy and eagerness.

- I can meet new opportunities without fear.

- Fearlessly, I face my fears.

- Today I have the courage to keep my dreams alive.

- I dare to be myself.

- Today I dare to be different, to live my own life and to follow my own heart.

- I remove my masks today and I reveal my genuine self.

- Today I step outside my comfort zone into new experiences and open myself to a fuller expression of living.

- Today I will take chances.

- I now take the first step toward my goal and the most exciting part of my life begins.

Task List and Action Plan

Before you go on to the next chapter, take time now to do these activities. They will help you get more out of the rest of this book.

- Review the table "How Self-Talk Affects Behavior." Do you identify with any of the rows? Can you add a few of your own?

- Write a list of people, places, and institutions that have most impacted your current values and beliefs.

- Practice being a filmmaker. The next time an event distresses you, see if there are alternative perspectives you can view the event from.

- Review the affirmations and put a check or star next to the ones that are important to you.

- Write the selected affirmations on a piece of notebook paper in your own handwriting.

- Choose one to five affirmations from your list and write them on index cards or Post-it notes. Put one on your bathroom mirror, one on your refrigerator, one on your dashboard, one at your bedside, and one on your desk.

6

Words at Work

Writing Effective Affirmations

In the previous chapter you were given a variety of affirmations to get started. However, it will be most effective if you to learn to write your own affirmations. As you grow and change you will no doubt encounter new challenges in life, some of which you can better handle with the use of positive self-talk. An affirmation helps to shift your focus from lack to possibility, from old to new. Affirmations help you to focus on what you want, not what you don't. What you focus your mental energy on dictates what you experience and attract. Affirmations make your thoughts work *for* you, not against you. For example, if you have a goal but you get off-track and don't do things perfectly, you can either focus on what a failure you've been or you can forgive yourself and refocus your energy. If you keep your focus on what you are striving for and on all of the progress you've made, it will be easier for you to get back on track.

An affirmation is a statement that clearly outlines what you desire. It should be personalized and specific and reflect what you hope to be true in the near future. Begin the affirmation with words such as "I" or "My." You can further personalize the affirmations by beginning with "I," followed by your name ("I, Sheri Zampelli . . ."). Although an affirmation outlines a condition you hope to have in the future, it should be stated in the present tense as if it is true now, such as "I am" or "I now have." Use the present tense to indicate that what you want is already here. If you act as if something is true, your mind will help you create a way to make it so. If you put your affirmation in the future tense, your mind will postpone the solution to some future date—but you want to start moving toward your goals now. Don't postpone your success by putting your affirmations in the future tense.

Another important thing to remember while formulating affirmations is to use positive words. For example, "able, competent, and capable," as opposed to negative words like "won't, try, and hate." For example, instead of saying "I won't overeat," say "I am eating less automatically." Instead of saying "I won't sit on my butt all day and be lazy," say "I am now motivated, enthusiastic, and energized." Put all of your focus on what you do want, not on what you don't want.

What if I were to tell you not to think about Easter eggs? What happens? Usually your mind instantly begins to think about Easter eggs. The same thing happens when you say "I won't smoke" or "I won't overeat"—your mind becomes focused on the very thing you don't want it to be focused on. Replace those thoughts with ideas like, "I enjoy clean air, fresh breath, and healthy lungs," or "I love it when my body is lean and healthy." Focus on the positive aspects of change versus the negative.

It's also helpful to use words that provoke emotion, enthusiasm, and excitement. You can change an affirmation such as "I am moving toward my goals" to "I am moving toward my goals with enthusiasm." Words that might help spice up your affirmation include:

- excitedly
- abundantly
- opulent
- soaring

- enthusiastically
- ecstatic
- boundless
- thrilled

- basking in
- exhilarated
- reveling in
- exuberant
- blissful
- gorgeous
- rapture
- exceptional
- celebration
- triumphant
- outrageously
- excellent
- enchanted
- tingly
- hilarious

It's important for you to choose words that are meaningful and effective for you. Rather than simply using affirmations that someone else has written, use them as a guideline to formulate your own. Be sure to choose appropriate words that mean what you want them to mean. A woman once told me she wanted more challenge in her career. She was feeling unmotivated and uninspired. She wanted to use her creativity so she wrote the following affirmation: "I am now involved in creative work that challenges me." She got challenged all right, but it wasn't the type of challenge she was looking for. Challenge can also mean struggle and hard work. Be sure you choose your words carefully and that you are aware of what the word means to you. The dictionary contains the official definitions to words, we have our own meanings linked to words as well. Sometimes your affirmations work extremely well so be careful what you ask for, because you just might get it.

Some people wonder if it's simply denial to make affirmations positive. Although it's not healthy to deny all negative feelings, once you distance yourself from the problem, you are able to look at it more objectively and find positive solutions. Feeling negativity from time to time is a normal experience, but in order to move away from negativity in your life you have to focus on the positive outcomes you desire.

Keeping Things Realistic

Effective affirmations must sound logical and not so far-fetched that our minds reject them before they have a chance to work. Writing affirmations that are too good to be true might be a form of self-sabotage. For example, if you want to overcome shyness you could say an affirmation like, "I am now confident and assertive in social situations." For some people this affirmation would work quite well, but for others it might be too far-fetched. If you are terrified of social situations and have difficulty maintaining a conversation, it might be nearly impossible for you to imagine being confident and assertive in social situations. There are a few things you can do to tone down this affirmation so that your mind will accept it.

Try using the word "becoming." For example, say "I am now becoming confident and assertive in social situations," so your mind cannot reject the idea as easily. You can also say, "I handle social situations effectively." Once you become comfortable with this idea and you've experienced some personal success, then you can change your affirmation to something a little bit more challenging.

In general, your affirmations should challenge your current beliefs and cause slight anxiety from breaking out of your comfort zone. You should have a sense that the affirmation is possible, but you don't have to be fully convinced or confident and you don't have to understand how the affirmation will come true. If your response to your affirmation is "This will never happen," you may need to tone it down until it seems feasible.

When working with weight loss clients, I taught how beliefs can affect your body. If you believe "I will always be fat," or "No matter what I eat I just keep getting fatter," this will become your truth. Clients were encouraged to tell themselves things like "I am naturally thin" or "My metabolism burns up all food rapidly." This worked well for some; however, other clients rejected the above affirmations. If an obese person uses these particular affirmations it might be so far from their true belief that they won't get any benefit. One solution to this dilemma is to use an intermediary affirmation like, "I am becoming thinner" or "I am on my way to a body that I enjoy." This affirmation will be more difficult for the mind to reject, and therefore will probably work more effectively.

A desolate person who wants to improve their financial situation probably shouldn't use an affirmation like, "I am a millionaire." Instead, "My financial situation is improving," or "I am increasing my income and decreasing my debt," is likely to be more effective. A person who wants to start college shouldn't start affirming "I have a Ph.D.," but might say, "I am smart, talented, and capable." "I am in the process of obtaining a higher education" might feel more feasible. Affirmations should challenge preexisting beliefs but not to the degree that the mind rejects them completely.

There are other, more complex forms of affirmations that you can learn about in various books. You may find very effective affirmations that go against the suggestions I have outlined. Some people choose to use quotes from famous people or religious quotations as an inspirational affirmation. The positive statements you use should make you feel hopeful and faithful. They should promote a feeling of inspiration and open your mind to new ways of thinking.

Affirmations and Avoidance

Affirmations work. They change beliefs, thereby altering behavior and impacting life events. It is common for a person to get so excited about the results of affirmation writing that they want to use affirmations to change or control all negative events in their lives. Be cautious. Positive affirmations shouldn't be used to avoid reality or hide from your feelings. It's normal to feel hurt, angry, or sad. You shouldn't try to avoid your feelings by using affirmations. Some people can use affirmations destructively, as one uses drugs and alcohol. If you use affirmations to stuff your feelings down and deny your pain, the affirmations will eventually stop working. Just like an addict or alcoholic's life becomes unmanageable as a result of substance abuse, your life can become unmanageable if you try to use affirmations to mask reality. We are better off facing things the way they really are, while also acknowledging that no matter what is going on in our outside world, we can control our inner reactions. With a positive mental attitude and an open mind, you'll be better able to find concrete solutions to your outside problems. This is where affirmations are valuable.

You can use affirmations to accept yourself exactly as you are. For example, if you are rageful and feel like lashing out, but you don't want to hurt others, you may decide to use affirmations to "get over" your negative emotions. This can be destructive if you don't deal with what caused the emotions in the first place. What might be more beneficial is to say an affirmation like, "I give myself permission to feel and express anger in healthy, constructive ways." This way you don't deny your feelings, but you also don't let self-destruction take over.

Dwelling on negativity rarely does any good, but neither does ignoring it. Ignoring or denying negativity actually gives it more power. Negative thoughts grow in the dark, so bring them into the light, examine them, see what you can do to change the situations behind them, and move on.

The Power of Repetition

Chances are you've spent many years reinforcing old, negative, limiting beliefs. These beliefs have become the truth for you. It will require repetition and reinforcement to replace old beliefs and institute new ideas into your schema.

In the beginning, positive affirmations may seem odd to you. You may feel like you're lying to yourself or you may find some affirmations hard to believe. You don't have to believe your affirmations in order for them to work. Once you begin working with them, your perceptions begin to change and you see things differently. The more you use them the more believable they become.

It's Like Learning a New Language

You can't just decide to become fluent in a new language and see instant results. In order to be proficient in a new language, you have to temporarily forget everything you've learned and be willing to see it in a new way. You may have noticed that people forget the foreign languages they've learned if they don't continue taking classes. In fact, people who were fully bilingual in childhood can forget one of the languages if they don't practice. By the same token, you will probably forget what you're learning in this book unless you apply it daily.

If you've lived your entire life thinking negative thoughts or feeling inferior or being punished for not being good enough, that's the language you know and relate to. But that doesn't make it right. In order to change the language you identify with, you will need to reinforce your new language consistently. You'll need to place yourself in settings where you will be surrounded by it. You will need to read books, listen to tapes, and/or practice aloud and silently. You'll need to change the way you communicate with others. It's no quick fix, but it does work if you put in the time and effort.

Think about things you would do if you wanted to learn a new language. Usually when a person embarks on a new language they spend hours and hours studying it. They listen to tapes, work with a tutor, watch movies in the foreign language, and write and rewrite newly learned words. They apply these new words to simple sentences, and slowly but gradually they add more difficulty to the task as they feel comfortable. This is the way you should approach your "new language" of success. Take your time. Start with easy affirmations. Practice them over and over until they begin to sound natural to you. Lay a solid foundation and be patient with yourself. You can't expect to learn a new language overnight. If you want to be fluent in a language you have to practice it daily. You have to use it in your everyday life or you will soon forget it.

Written Affirmations

Your current belief system is habitual. Therefore you'll need to take extra steps in the beginning to break your old habits and replace them with new ways of thinking and behaving. It will be helpful to develop routines or rituals to remind you of your new self-talk and make it more natural. An affirmation journal is a good way to get started. Affirmation journals are simple to use and inexpensive. It might prove to be the cheapest form of therapy available. All you need is a notebook and a pen. Dedicate about fifteen minutes in the morning and in the evening to writing your new affirmations. You can use affirmations that you've chosen from this book or those you've written on your own. Write at least one full page of affirmations (front and back). If you have less than a full page of unique affirmations, continue writing the same ones over and over until you have filled a page. Rewrite this page of affirmations twice a day. This will help you wake up with positive thoughts first thing in the morning and set a positive tone for the day. You'll also go to sleep with positive thoughts, which can positively affect your dreams. Reading done prior to retiring at night is better retained. Study skills textbooks often recommend studying difficult subjects right before going to bed.

Writing helps you stay focused. It's harder to become distracted while writing than it is while thinking. When you write affirmations you are using the kinesthetic, visual, and auditory parts of your brain. You are simultaneously engaging your hand, mind, and eyes. You are also saying the affirmations to yourself as you write them. Engaging several portions of your brain at once allows the affirmation to sink in at a deeper level. Creating a ritual of writing affirmations daily helps you to form a new habit. If possible, do this work at the same time every day so it can become part of your routine.

You'll want to keep writing and rewriting these affirmations until they start to feel natural to you. Once you've internalized an affirmation, you can change it to something new and more challenging. The best indication that it's time to move on to a new affirmation is when you see results in your life that coincide with your affirmation. Thirty minutes of positive affirmations per day can make a tremendous difference in your life.

In addition to writing your affirmations in a journal, choose a couple of your most important affirmations and transfer them over to index cards. Place your written affirmations (on index cards or post-it notes) in easy-to-remember locations so you can read them repeatedly each day. You can place them on your walls and mirrors at home and on your desk at work. Put them on your refrigerator, in your car or your wallet, or anywhere else you will see them on a daily basis. You may also be able to put an affirmation on your computer's screensaver. If you don't want other people to see your affirmations, you can place a colored dot in various locations and tell yourself, "Each time I see this colored dot I will say my affirmations."

Anytime you catch yourself in negative, demeaning, worrisome, or critical self-talk, stop yourself immediately and replace your negative thoughts with affirmations. Use positive self-talk as often as possible during the day, even when you aren't aware of negative self-talk. Eventually the positive ideas will sink in and you will see miracles happening in your life.

Audio Affirmations

Endless-loop cassette tapes or homemade CDs are a powerful way to reinforce new beliefs. Once you've developed a list of affirmations that address your goals and dreams, record them onto a cassette and listen to them daily. Cassettes are a portable and powerful tool for self-transformation. You can listen to them as you get ready for work, as you drive in the car, and as you cook, clean, shave, and work out at the gym. Use all "down time" as an opportunity to reinforce your new beliefs. You can use regular cassette tapes for your affirmations, though I highly recommend you use endless-loop cassette tapes or CDs. These formats allow you to listen to your affirmations with little effort. You don't have to turn them over, nor do you have to rewind, or fast-forward them. Simply press play and you're in business.

An endless cassette tape continues in a loop with no beginning or ending and is available in lengths from thirty seconds to twenty minutes. The tape has no leader to indicate where it stops or ends so it plays continually. If you record thirty seconds worth of affirmations on an endless cassette and then press play, that cassette will continue to play forever, until you press the stop button. Endless cassettes are usually found at musician supply and electronics stores. Be sure to follow the manufacturer's directions carefully for best results. Homemade CDs are another tool to use. Once you make your CD, you can use the repeat function on your player to listen to your affirmations nonstop.

Your affirmations can become even more effective when written as a jingle. Advertisers have long used catchy jingles and repetition to plant thoughts in our minds to affect our buying behavior. You can use the same techniques that cost advertisers billions of dollars. You can use repetition to your advantage by making an affirmation jingle and recording it on an endless-loop tape. You can also play music in the background as you record your affirmation tape so the affirmations really seep into your consciousness. With continued use, you will find yourself humming your affirmations or saying them to yourself—even when you aren't listening to the tape.

You can turn off your radio during commercials and use endless cassettes or CDs in your car so that you're listening to your affirmations instead of commercials. Some commercial breaks are as long as ten minutes. Why not use this time to promote your own cause by listening to your affirmation tapes?

You can also make mellow, soothing tapes and play them all night long so that the last thing you hear before retiring and the first thing you hear upon awakening is positive. Research shows that your subconscious mind is awake even as you sleep. Patients who undergo surgery or become unconscious are able to recall details of what was said and what type of music was played during surgery. If you play your tape continuously while you sleep, a part of your mind will hear it, making it even more effective.

Once you have listened to endless tapes for about a month or so and have them memorized, you can play them at a very low, almost inaudible volume and still "hear" them. Have you ever noticed that when a car passes with the stereo turned up and you catch a part of a song that you know, you automatically get it stuck in your mind and finish singing it, even though the car is long gone? Also, if you know a song well, you can "hear" it quite well with the volume turned down whereas you cannot hear an unfamiliar song at the same volume. This is because your mind is filling in the blanks based on past experience. The same thing can happen with your affirmation tapes or CDs.

I often play my endless cassette tapes at a low volume in my house while I work, eat, watch TV, and sleep. Sometimes I forget to turn them off when people visit. Some visitors don't hear the tape at all, while others ask me, "What's that noise?" They cannot hear the tape or decipher what it's saying, they can only hear that there is something on. However, I can hear the tape quite well. As I move from room to room and pass my cassette player, I will catch bits and pieces of the affirmations, but my mind will continue the thought as I walk into the next room.

Using Affirmations as a Learning Tool

You can use affirmations to help you identify some of your reasons for resisting change. Many people say things like: "I believe that I deserve a good relationship and I think I am a good person, but I still keep attracting the wrong relationships into my life." There's a difference between conscious thought and unconscious thought. In our conscious mind we may believe that we are good people with much to offer, but subconsciously we might be holding on to old fears, failures, and programming that says, "You're not good enough, no one will love you exactly as you are."

For example, if you think of yourself as a person with high self-esteem and strong boundaries, yet you continually attract people who take advantage of you, it's possible that there's a part of you that's not convinced of your worth. If you feel convinced that you deserve good things yet you never have them, there may be a part of you that feels undeserving or fearful of good things. The "Root Down Worksheet" at the end of this chapter can help you identify subconscious beliefs. Begin by taking out a piece of paper and folding it in half lengthwise. On the left side of the page, write an affirmation about an area of your life you want to work on. For example, if your goal is to make a career change, your affirmation would be something like, "I am now moving in the direction of my ideal career." On the right side of the page, keep track of the thoughts or feelings you encounter after you write or say the initial affirmation. For example, after writing the above affirmation, you might say to yourself, "Yeah, right, I'm not moving anywhere," or you might get a feeling of anxiety in your gut—write these verbal and nonverbal reactions down in the right column.

It's important that you write down your first reaction. Don't write what you think you should write. Write what you truly think and feel. Writing down these awarenesses is one way to learn why you are resisting change. Writing down your negative thoughts doesn't mean you have to buy into them or take them seriously, you can simply use them to learn more about yourself. Having them down on paper helps take the power from them. For example, if your reaction to the career affirmation was one of anxiety, you now know that you are fearful about changing careers. So the issue is no longer career change but your fear of it. You can then redirect your efforts and your affirmations toward focusing on stress reduction and a stress-free career change. Change your affirmation to "I now have the courage to change careers, everything I need to make this change is attracted to me easily and effortlessly." If this new affirmation brings up a new concern, address that with a different affirmation. Continue this process until you are no longer writing negative, fearful responses in the second column. Use your newly formed affirmation until it becomes comfortable to you. Once you feel ready to move forward, choose a new affirmation that slightly challenges your current belief system but is feasible and realistic.

Sue believed that her problems stemmed from low self-esteem and low self-worth, so she might write an affirmation like, "I am willing to release the need to be unworthy. I am worthy of the very best in life and I now lovingly allow myself to accept that truth." If her internal reaction to this affirmation was something like, "I'm not worthy. I'm fat, ugly, and stupid, I don't deserve anything good. Even when I do get good things, I just screw them up anyway. I'm a loser. I'll never change," she would then have some realizations as to why she felt unworthy. First of all, she thinks she is fat, ugly, and stupid. So she should write affirmations that reflect the opposite of that belief. She could say, "I am worthy of good things despite my weight and appearance," "As my inner vision of myself changes, so does the outer vision," or "I am becoming more beautiful each and every day."

Sue needs to take each of these statements and focus on their opposites, formulating new affirmations. For example, she can change "I am a loser" to "I am a winner," change "I always mess things up" to "I accept all good that comes to me because it is mine and I deserve it." Finally, she can reverse "I will never change" to "I am now in the process of change."

As you fill out the "Root Down Worksheet," continue writing positive affirmations in the left column and then the response in the right column until you feel you have cleared out the negativity and identified the main beliefs that stand in your way. Remember to write and/or say your new affirmations daily.

Following is an example of a root down exercise written by Geneva, a woman who was very successful when selling products and services for someone else but felt fearful when it came to promoting herself. She wanted to stop making money for everyone else and start her own business.

Affirmation	Response
I am now learning to sell myself rather than selling others. I'm ready to succeed.	How selfish can you be? You're stuck on yourself. It's too hard to sell yourself. Who are you trying to fool?
I take care of myself and allow others to take care of themselves. We are all becoming stronger.	You're too old for all of this. Why don't you just stick with what you know? You're good at promoting others, why change now?
I give myself credit for the hard work I've done. I know I can do what I put my mind to.	Yeah, but you're old. By the time you get things going, you'll have to retire. Why not stick with what you know?
I am willing to try new things. I can learn and grow at any age.	Who do you think you are?
I'm a strong, talented, and determined woman.	I'll say, you're a hard head.
I use my skills to my benefit.	

By the time Geneva got to the end of this exercise she had nothing to put in the response column. She felt stronger about her ability and saw her attitude as an asset to future success. She truly believed nothing could stop her and she moved forward on her new goal with greater confidence than ever.

Focus on the Facts

If you have trouble with positive thinking, make an effort to distract yourself from the negative. If you are unable to focus on positive aspects of a situation, make an attempt to focus on something besides negativity. Perhaps you can call a friend or read a good book. Maybe you can go for a walk or do some other form of exercise. Although it's not healthy to deny all negative feelings, once you distance yourself from the problem, you are able to look at it more objectively and find positive solutions. Feeling negative from time to time is a normal experience, but you don't have to let it get the best of you.

If distracting yourself doesn't work, try focusing on the facts. Focusing on the facts is an intermediary step that enables you to take the emotion and power out of negative, self-defeating thoughts. For example, instead of saying, "I'm so lazy, I can't believe it's Sunday and I still haven't done any of the errands I told myself I'd do," state the facts and say, "It's Sunday and I haven't accomplished everything on my list of things to do. I still have time to do a few things." That is all that is factual, the rest is judgment and opinion. These judgments and opinions don't help you feel better or reach your goals.

If you are angry at your partner you could think, "That creep doesn't even care about me. Look at him, he's ignoring me, I bet he's having an affair. Well, who needs that? I'll show him." These thoughts may or may not be true, but dwelling on them makes you feel worse and won't lead you to wise, healthy decision making. Turn your thoughts around and focus on the facts. It might look something like this: "My partner is not listening to me and I am angry." This new statement takes the power out of negativity and gives it back to you. Now you can decide what action to take. You can choose to remain angry, you can discuss the situation with your partner, you could write about it—there are many steps you can take that will remedy the situation and help you feel better. Once you have toned down your negative self-talk by focusing on the facts, you can then use positive affirmations more effectively.

Written Dialogue: Changing Your Perspective

A written dialogue can help heighten your awareness of the self-defeating thoughts that hold you back. This is a free-flowing journaling exercise to help you gain new perspectives on troubling situations. This technique is particularly helpful when you are feeling depressed, stuck, afraid, or frustrated about your progress. Begin by stating what's on your mind. Write how you feel. Then switch roles and write a response to your frustration taking a different perspective. For example, let's say you want to stop working for an employer and start your own business. Perhaps you've tried many things but you never quite get to the point where you can quit your job. You feel frustrated and feel like a failure. Your written dialogue might go something like this: "I'm so sick of my job, I wish I could start my own business. Every time I try, something happens to set me back. First it was my car breaking down, then it was my daughter's braces. I'll never get ahead. I was a fool to think that I could."

After you've written out your frustration, take a different perspective such as, "Maybe part of the problem is that I don't budget my money well. Maybe if I set a budget and set aside money in savings, these life events wouldn't set me back so far." Continue this dialogue until you've reached some sort of resolution within yourself or come up with a potential solution or plan of action. The negative comments you wrote out can also provide you with direction for future affirmations. The following is an example of how you can break down the frustration sentences and turn each one into an affirmation.

Frustration Statement	New Affirmation
I'm sick of my job.	I give thanks for employment.
I wish I could start my own business.	I am now guided and directed towards everything I need to start my own business.

Every time I try, something happens to set me back.	I am moving forward, I am overcoming all obstacles toward my goals.
I'll never get ahead.	I am moving forward and progressing each and every day.
I am a fool.	I am wise, smart, guided, and inspired to take the right action to move me toward my goal.

Say Good-bye to Self-Sabotage

A good-bye letter to negative self-talk can help you gain a sense of control. This is like a "Dear John" letter to the negative voice that has held you back. It can help you realize that you have control over negative self-talk. Negative self-talk is only a portion of you, it is not all of you. Why not imagine that this negative voice or saboteur is a bully who you've allowed to pick on you for years. Today you have the opportunity to take back your power and stand up to that bully once and for all. Imagine that this bully is on one of your shoulders, whispering unkind words into your ear and on your other shoulder is an angel of positive self-talk. Then, imagine just flicking that bully off of your shoulder or telling it where to go. Here are some examples of good-bye letters:

> Dear Saboteur,
>
> You've held me back for long enough. You've lied to me and I've been believing you, but now is the time I am going to take back my power. You have prevented me from living my life to the fullest, and life is too short for that. I am going to take charge of my life. Good-bye.

> Hello, Low Self-Esteem,
>
> You've been with me all my life. As long as I can remember, I've carried you around. I've believed in you, I've pampered you, I've given you control of me. I've let you trash my life. I've let you darken my outlook. I've worshipped you, even. And for what? You've never helped me. You've always put me down. You've fulfilled your promise of darkness and misery, but now you're free! Now you can go your way—I'm going my way without you. Too bad for you. No longer burden me with your trash. I'm living my life now and without you. You're gone. Good-bye.

> Dear Fear,
>
> Today I say good-bye to you with great joy. You came into my life like the fog into the night, slowly creeping and growing thicker and thicker until you consumed everything around and in your path. I

look back into my life with great remorse and regret that I ever let you in. Tears come to my eyes when I think of all the good memories of my life you've torn to shreds. I have never been one to let go of anyone or anything easily, but today I will let go of you and say good-bye with all that I am, all that I ever was, and all that I could be. You see me as weak, I see myself as strong without you. Forever I will go on.

A good-bye letter to your self-defeating thoughts and behavior can be incredibly freeing. I've seen workshop participants light up and grin widely after writing one of these letters. At times, willing participants read their letters aloud and the room takes on a festive feel. Some participants have made songs and poems to say good-bye to the saboteur. A letter like this can lift the weight of negativity and depression and give you a sense of empowerment.

Some of us have been carrying around the same old negative beliefs for many years. We may have been criticized or belittled by our parents or partner, and somewhere along the line we internalized the demeaning messages and began to say them to ourselves. An exercise like this can help you realize that you don't have to listen to the negative, critical voice anymore. You can stop reinforcing the negativity anytime you choose. It may not be easy, but it is possible to change.

Task List and Action Plan

Before you go on to the next chapter, take time now to do these activities. They will help you get more out of the rest of this book.

- Read the "Writing an Effective Affirmation" worksheet that follows. Make up some of your own and compare them to the checklist at the bottom of the worksheet.

- Write out a full page of affirmations.

- Choose one to ten of these and put them on index cards or post-it notes in easy-to-see places.

- Place reminders to motivate you to use your new self-talk.

- Record your affirmations on a cassette or CD. Listen to them daily.

- Use the "Affirmation Tracking Worksheet" to keep track of the work you do daily (i.e., how many affirmations you write, how many minutes you listened to the tape, how many times you read your posted affirmations).

- During the next week, take note of your negative, fatalistic thinking and practice focusing on the facts.

- Do the root down exercise and continue to heighten your awareness of the negative, limiting thoughts that hold you back.

- Do a written dialogue.

- Write a good-bye letter to your saboteur. Read it aloud.

Writing an Effective Affirmation

One way to begin changing your negative self-talk and opening your mind to new possibilities is to use positive affirmations. Repetition, patience, reinforcement, and time are the keys to making affirmations work. Below are some guidelines for writing effective positive affirmations.

1. Start with "I" or "My." You can also use your name.

2. Keep it in the present tense: am, is, have, am becoming, am willing, choose, etc.

3. State what you want to become: deserving, worthwhile, valuable, capable, etc.

Examples:
"I deserve good things."
"I like myself."
"I accept myself."

Try to avoid using negative words. Instead of saying, "I won't procrastinate," try: "I now use my time wisely. I complete projects in a timely manner."

Avoid using vague language like "I will." We can say, "I will," for the rest of our lives, but when will we?

More examples:
"I believe in myself."
"I am capable."
"I am changing my negative habits into positive ones."

As you become more comfortable with affirmation writing you can get more creative. Just remember the basics: personalized statements, present tense, positive words, and words that evoke positive feelings in you.

More examples:
"I have the audacity to live my dreams."
"I am triumphant over negative, self-destructive thinking."

Use a blank page to write out some of your own affirmations, use the following checklist to evaluate their effectiveness:

_____ Is it positive?

_____ Is it in the present tense?

_____ Does it use descriptive words?

_____ Does it get you out of your comfort zone?

_____ Does it accurately state what you desire?

_____ Is it specific?

Affirmation Tracking Worksheet

Week of: _____

Day One:	Yes/No	How many times/How long
said affirmations aloud		
wrote affirmations in a journal		
read posted affirmations		
listened to affirmation tape		

Day Two	Yes/No	How many times/How long
said affirmations aloud		
wrote affirmations in a journal		
read posted affirmations		
listened to affirmation tape		

Day Three	Yes/No	How many times/How long
said affirmations aloud		
wrote affirmations in a journal		
read posted affirmations		
listened to affirmation tape		

Day Four	Yes/No	How many times/How long
said affirmations aloud		
wrote affirmations in a journal		
read posted affirmations		
listened to affirmation tape		

Day Five	Yes/No	How many times/How long
said affirmations aloud		
wrote affirmations in a journal		
read posted affirmations		
listened to affirmation tape		

Day Six	Yes/No	How many times/How long
said affirmations aloud		
wrote affirmations in a journal		
read posted affirmations		
listened to affirmation tape		

Day Seven	Yes/No	How many times/How long
said affirmations aloud		
wrote affirmations in a journal		
read posted affirmations		
listened to affirmation tape		

Use the space below to write down observations or awarenesses that occurred from working with your affirmations.

_____

_____

_____

_____

_____

_____

_____

Root Down Worksheet

Affirmation	Response

7

See It, Believe It, Make It Real

"Seeing" is more than physical eyesight. In fact, many times seeing requires closing your eyes to reality. It means looking beyond outside appearances and being willing to expand your vision to include your innermost dreams and desires, even if they seem unrealistic and impossible. Can you imagine, envision, and describe your desire? Can you talk about it with a friend? Can you see it in your mind's eye? If you can't see your dream life vividly right now, keep reading and you can learn the skills you need to do so.

Believing in something means having faith. It means expecting cooperation and results. Sometimes faith is based on nothing more than inner intuition. To believe something means to accept it without question. When gardeners plant a seed, they don't dig it up every day to see how well it's growing—they leave it in the ground with the expectation that since they planted a seed, they will someday see a plant. Your beliefs and dreams are manifested with the same precision. If you plant seeds of lack, limitation, disharmony, and fear, that's what you'll grow. If you plant seeds of hope, determination, desire, and motivation, and nurture them each day, that's what you'll harvest.

Beliefs and ideas have power. Everything starts as an idea and then becomes reality. Business ventures, marriage proposals, college degrees, and success all begin with an idea, a vision. All it takes is for someone to believe in an idea enough to act on making it become a reality.

Making an idea real comes as a result of seeing and believing. You don't have to understand how something will become real in order to get started. Chances are, your ideas are much more limited than the array of actual opportunities you will encounter. Dare to open your mind to the endless possibilities of life. Know that your human perception is limited. You can't predict all the possible outcomes of a situation. Many factors such as the neighborhood you grew up in; your socioeconomic status; the era you grew up in; influences from your parents, teachers, friends, and the media; your gender; your religion; and your race all affect your perception. None of us can predict the totality of possibilities.

Creative Daydreaming

We all daydream. Sometimes we imagine the ideal wedding ceremony or we imagine going to our high school reunion and showing off our success. Sometimes we imagine a perfect Hawaiian vacation or what we'd do if we won the lottery. These daydreams are fun, and for the most part, harmless. Other times we have less pleasant daydreams such as being robbed or getting into a car accident. Again, these can be harmless depending on the degree to which we let them run our lives. They are fantasy, not necessarily based on our own real-life experiences.

The third type of daydreaming isn't usually referred to as such. This is our negative rehearsal session. This is when the day before a test we "practice" failing by telling ourselves, "I'll never pass that test. I should have studied more." Maybe we can actually imagine ourselves sitting in our desk, looking at the test and freezing up, not knowing any of the answers. Another example is practicing failure at a job interview or a first date or a presentation we are scheduled to handle. When we daydream failure, we are engaging in negative self-talk and negative self-imaging. Affirmations can be a great help to us at this time, but creative daydreaming can help us even more.

Creative daydreaming is a tool you can use to visualize yourself as a successful person. It can help keep your focus on your desired end result. Instead of mentally practicing failure prior to attempting a difficult and unfamiliar task, you can take time to quiet yourself, close your eyes, and imagine total success. In creative day-dreaming you can imagine a well-received speech, a compatible date, or a stress-free exam in full, rich, vivid detail—thereby gearing up your mind and body for success instead of failure.

There are two ways to use creative daydreaming. The first is structured day-dreaming, during which you set aside some quiet time by yourself and close your eyes. Take in two to three deep breaths and let your thoughts become less frantic. Once you have calmed down a bit, imagine a time when you were totally successful. Relax completely and try to imagine what success felt like to you. How were you car-rying yourself? What was the weather like? What were you wearing? Who else was with you? What did your surroundings look like? Smell like? Sound like? Next, think about a goal you would like to attain. Imagine in vivid detail that you have achieved your goal and you feel great. Mentally practice success and the rewards that come with it. Focus your mental energy on total success for several minutes. After you open your eyes, carry that feeling of success with you into the rest of the day.

You can also use creative daydreaming anytime during the day. When you find yourself focusing on negative daydreams and imagining tragic outcomes, stop your-self immediately and replace the daydream with a positive outcome. The subcon-scious mind loves exaggeration, so go ahead and vividly imagine success. Take your daydream from tragedy to triumph.

Use creative daydreaming to imagine a situation turning out as you wish. Focus on what it will be like to be in a healthy relationship or have a career you love. Focus on how good it feels to live in a clutter-free environment, accomplish goals, and improve self-esteem. Creative daydreaming can help you keep sight of your purpose.

Mentoring: If They Can Do It, So Can You

You can use your creative daydreaming time to sit quietly and imagine all the people you know who have accomplished the goal you desire to attain. As you imagine the success of others, remind yourself, "If they can do it, so can I." You don't have to know these individuals personally, simply make a list of all people, dead or alive, who've accomplished the goal you desire to accomplish. Then use the list as evidence that your goal is possible. You might even imagine yourself walking around in the body of someone you admire. Imagine yourself in the same position, being success-ful. In Napoleon Hill's book, *Think and Grow Rich*, he recommends calling a mental meeting with sources of guidance to see how they might handle a particular situation (1972). For example, you might want to ask Martin Luther King, Jr., or Isadora

Duncan to guide you or give you advice. Use your imagination to visualize their presence and imagine what they might say.

A mentor is someone who has been successful in the area of life in which you'd like to succeed. If you can't think of anyone who has achieved the goal you desire, try to think of clubs, organizations, or corporations that these people would be likely to frequent. If your mentor is alive, do all you can to contact them. Call, write, e-mail, or fax them. When looking for a mentor, you may have to call, write, or approach people you don't know. This can feel like a tremendous risk, but you'll be surprised how many people will help you.

Remember, what you say is what you get. Be sure to approach these mentors with an attitude of openness and expectation. If you contact them with an attitude like, "I doubt you want to help me," or "I know you're too busy," you'll probably get exactly what you expect: nothing. Instead, have a positive attitude when you contact people. When you ask someone for help you're paying them a huge compliment. Some people will be flattered, appreciated, and honored that you admire their work. You may not always get a positive response, but if you continue trying, eventually you will find someone who can help you.

Spending time with people you admire can help you raise your expectations and challenge limiting ideas. It can help you break out of your cycle of believing it's hard to change, grow, and succeed. Watching other people who are doing what you want to do can be helpful in learning new behaviors. If, for example, you want to learn more about a particular computer program, talk to someone who has mastered it. If you want to write a book, talk to a published author. Sometimes you can save yourself years of work by learning from the experiences and mistakes of others. Ask mentors what they do to succeed. Better yet, watch them in action, because some of the things they do may be so automatic to them that they don't realize they're doing them.

Reading books about famous people or those who have accomplished your desired goals can be helpful. As read biographies, look for and focus on the similarities you share with others. You'll notice that all people have struggles to contend with. No one has it easy or gets all the breaks. All people, famous and rich included, have struggles. The difference between a successful person and an unsuccessful person is how they handle struggle. Most successful people have learned to make lemonade out of lemons and to turn obstacles into opportunities. This is something you can learn to do as well. If your thought pattern says that successful, happy people are somehow luckier or better than you, break out of it. Look for commonalties and you will find them. When you read stories, try to look at them from the perspective of, "If they can do it, so can I."

Another thing you'll realize when you read these books is that there are many roads to success and many exceptions to the rules. Sometimes we make up rules about how success must be obtained. These rules provide us with excuses as to why we can't succeed. For example, you may believe in a rule like: You have to have connections to get ahead. And if you don't have connections, you may believe that you can't get ahead. Books about successful people will show you that success has been attained by people with every imaginable kind of background. The rules to success and failure are really contained in our own minds.

Brainstorming to Expand Your Consciousness

If you're not sure what your goals are or how you can achieve them, brainstorm with others to come up with alternatives to your familiar beliefs. Ask yourself, "What are some of the things I can do to accomplish my goal?" Write down any answer that comes to your mind, no matter how crazy it seems. Don't judge your brainstorming. You can also find your own answers by taking a few deep breaths, closing your eyes for ten to fifteen minutes and repeating the following sentence to yourself: "I am clear and receptive. I am ready for my highest good."

When you are sure what your goals are but not sure how to attain them, repeat this sentence: "I may not know how this is possible, but it is possible." Then remain quiet for about ten to fifteen minutes, allowing ideas to come to you naturally. Try not to judge, criticize, or analyze the thoughts that come, just observe them casually and note how creative and interesting they are. Don't get upset with yourself or try to force the thoughts out of your mind, because that just gives them more power. When distracting or negative thoughts come to your mind, simply allow them to drift away naturally.

You may want to put a pen and paper by your side before you start this process so that you can write down any ideas or inspirations that come your way. After the time is up, write down your ideas and then follow through on those that you are able to. Before you start, you may want to set a timer or play a fifteen-minute music tape so you'll know when the time is up without having to open your eyes and look at a clock.

Even if you don't get a great flash of inspiration from this exercise right away, it will work better as you continue. Sitting quietly and allowing yourself to relax can open your mind because you are less stressed and tense. The affirmation, "I may not know how this is possible, but it is possible," will help to open your mind to new possibilities. You may get ideas and inspirations after your meditation time, when you're doing something like driving your car or standing in line at a grocery store. Pay attention to these inspirations and dare to act on them, even if they sometimes seem silly. You never know what might happen if you make that phone call, pay that compliment, or send that letter.

Visualizing Your Ideal Future

The first step toward successful visualization is getting rid of any limiting ideas that you're holding on to regarding your ability to visualize. For the next moment, think of a telephone. What did you see? You probably pictured a telephone in your mind. It doesn't matter how vividly you imagined this object. As long as you got an outline, idea, or sense of a telephone, you can use visualization. Now try to imagine the following objects:

- beach

- candle

- zebra

- apple

Were you able to see these items in your mind's eye? Close your eyes right now and try to remember what your bedroom looks like. Can you see it? If so, you are capable of using visualization.

Perhaps you use visualization to help you remember the directions to a location you've been to before. Perhaps you've used it while studying or trying to remember something. Have you ever tried to give directions to a location and found you can't remember the exact address or the names of the streets, but you can remember what's on the corner and where you need to turn left or right? That's an example of visualization. Have you ever wanted to find a quote in a book and you can't remember the page number or the chapter but you do remember that it was somewhere midway in the book on the left-hand side in the last paragraph? That is also a form of visualization.

Visualization is a powerful tool used by actors, athletes, and businesspeople to produce outstanding results. Many championship athletes have boasted of increased performance after imaging success in their minds and practicing mentally. In fact, the mental training is at least as important, if not more so, than the physical training. In his book *Spiritual Economics*, Eric Butterworth tells of a research study conducted at the University of Chicago that tested the impact of visualization in the improvement of basketball scores. Participants were divided into three groups. Group one was given no training or help with improving basketball skills. They were told to go home and forget all about the study. Group two was told to practice shooting hoops one hour each day for thirty days, and group three was told to imagine themselves shooting hoops for one hour per day for the next thirty days. At the end of the thirty-day trial, the visualizers had improved twenty-three percent, only 1 percent less than those who practiced daily in the gym.

I was very intrigued by this study the first time I read it. To this day I wonder what would happen if a group practiced with the ball and visualized success at the same time.

Some terminally ill people have also used visualization to manage pain and promote healing and recovery in their bodies. I once read a story about a child who imagined that his cancer was a monster and his natural defenses were white knights. He used visualization to put his cancer into remission. What you focus on tends to become your reality, so it's to your advantage to focus on positive thoughts and success.

Make Your Own Advertisement

Display advertising has been extremely successful in affecting our buying behavior, whether we realize it or not. Advertisers spend billions of dollars a year strategically placing billboards, bus signs, and magazine ads in the right places so that we'll want to purchase the products we see advertised. It's time for us to make our own advertisements and decide for ourselves what we want to "buy." Advertising is not nearly as effective the first time we see it as it is the second, third, twentieth, or fiftieth time. Perhaps the first time we see a new product we might think it is stupid, silly, or that we're happy with what we already have. However, after repeated exposure, we may become curious, "sold" on the idea of this products' usefulness and willing to give it a try.

Our negative, self-defeating thoughts have been reinforced over many years. Perhaps we learned them at an early or vulnerable stage of our lives. We've come to accept them without question and they seem natural to us. Had we developed a strong and positive sense of self early on and maintained it throughout the years, we would see the absurdity of beliefs like, "I'm not worthy," or "I don't deserve success." We would be less likely to put up with verbal, emotional, or physical abuse from others. In psychology they've done experiments with frogs in beakers of water. If they place a frog directly in boiling water it will jump out immediately and be saved. If they place the same frog in water that is room temperature and gradually increase the temperature to boiling, the frog will comfortably sit awaiting it's own demise. In the same way, our negative ideas about ourselves have been built up slowly, perhaps preventing us from noticing how much these ideas are hurting us. But you don't have to be a passive recipient to other people's programming. You can decide for yourself what thoughts and ideas you focus on.

We must use repetition consciously and to our advantage. We can decide to be alert and keep our focus on beliefs that empower us rather than make us weak. Daily reinforcement of new ideas can help us to build our inner strength and overcome negative messages from the past.

Beneficial Billboard

You might not be able to avoid advertisements, but you can use the tool of visual display to your advantage. You can make a beneficial billboard. Your beneficial billboard can work like a multimillion dollar ad campaign, yet the whole project can be very inexpensive, depending on what materials you currently have available to you.

A beneficial billboard is a collage that contains words, phrases, and pictures that remind you of your goals and dreams. It's a hands-on creative project that awakens your subconscious mind to new possibilities. To begin, you'll need a poster board, glue, and a stack of magazines. Set aside some time to sort through the magazines and cut out words and pictures that represent your goals.

If you want to travel to Hawaii, cut out pictures of Hawaii, cut out the word Hawaii, cut out pictures of people eating, swimming, snorkeling, or sunbathing in Hawaii—anything that represents the things that you want to manifest in your life. You can also cut out pictures that symbolize your goals. For example, if you want more self-esteem, you can cut out pictures that symbolize self-esteem to you. A cat can be symbolic of self-esteem and self-autonomy. A bald eagle can symbolize rarity, beauty, strength, and clear vision. You can choose any picture that symbolizes values you want to focus your attention on.

You can either make a different beneficial billboard for each area of your life, or you can section your poster board off and focus on several different areas at once.

Use colorful poster board that evokes a feeling of lightness and positivity and avoid clustering your pictures too close together. Space your pictures enough so it's easy to focus on each one individually. As an experiment, you can look through magazines for a little while just to see what type of ad captures your attention. What's your style? What type of art do you enjoy? Use what already works for you so that your beneficial billboard will be enjoyable to look at.

Once you have designed your beneficial billboard, put it some place where you'll be able to see it on a regular basis. Look at it daily and allow the pictures to come to life for you. Imagine yourself doing, being, and having all the elements of your beneficial billboard. As you imagine this vividly, your mind will open the way for these dreams to become your reality. In the beginning, you may doubt that it's going to work, but don't give up. Look at your beneficial billboard every day until it becomes comfortable for you to think of yourself as a person who is worthy and capable of your goals.

At first you might think, "I don't really need to go to there," or "How will I ever have time to do these things?" But with repeated exposure to your new goals, change begins to feel more and more feasible. You'll begin to feel comfortable with this new idea—and maybe you'll even feel driven to accomplish it. This is the power of repetition working in your favor.

The Self-Fulfilling Scrapbook

Self-fulfilling scrapbooks are based on the same concept as beneficial billboards. Rather than putting your goals on a poster board, you put them in a book. You can use a notebook, scrapbook, or photo album. Use a book with removable pages so you can move pictures around at will (e.g., a three-ring album with magnetic pages). As you work with this book, you'll undoubtedly want to add and delete pictures. Your goals will start coming true and you won't need to focus on them as intently. You also might decide to change your goals, realizing that your original goal wasn't quite right for you.

It can be discouraging to spend hours on a project and not be able to change it later. You might not feel like doing a whole new book every time your goals change or every time you accomplish something. However, don't throw away the pages that represent accomplished goals; instead, keep them as a reminder that the self-fulfilling scrapbook really works. You should designate one page to each aspect of your life you want to improve. You might have one section for career, one for health, one for education, one for hobbies, and one for relationships. Some of the pages might contain a visual display of short-term goals (such as updating your resume, spending an hour cleaning out your closet, or asking someone out on a date). Other pages might have longer term goals such as getting married or buying a new home. Most importantly, choose pictures and words that vividly symbolize your goals.

Take time to find pictures that really get you motivated and make you feel excited and anticipatory. Avoid using small, drab, colorless, or worn-out pictures. Once you've designed a self-fulfilling scrapbook, set aside time to review it daily. Allow the pictures to come alive in your imagination. If you believe that it's possible for you to have all of these things in your life, you will have them.

Bring some fun into the project and look through the self-fulfilling scrapbook as if it's the future and you're looking back on all of the things you've done in life. Pretend you're thinking about old times, just like you probably do now with old photos of your family and friends. Acting as if the goals depicted in your scrapbook have already come true can focus your mind on how to make them happen. Choose a supportive friend who you trust and share your album with him or her. Pretend you're going over memories and say things like: "This is a picture from when I went to the Bahamas, and look, here's a picture of my house in Arizona."

When we were children we had no problem playing grown-up, daring to daydream and make up fun scenarios. As adults we can become too logical for our own good. We often get stuck in our roles and forget to have fun. Try not to take yourself too seriously. You don't have to know all the details of how you'll accomplish your goals. If you put the intention out there and focus on it daily, ideas and inspirations will come to you in unexpected ways. Someday that self-fulfilling scrapbook will be a true record of the things you've done in your life. You will look at it five to ten years from now and realize that it came true, it's on its way to coming true, or it didn't come true—but something even better happened instead.

As you look at your self-fulfilling scrapbook or beneficial billboard each day, you'll probably start to experience small changes in your thinking and your behavior. As time passes, you'll see yourself moving closer and closer to your goals without much stress or strain. You have absolutely nothing to lose from this practice and quite a bit to gain, so give it a try!

The Creating History Journal

Another positive tool to use while visualizing your desired goals is a creating history journal. In this journal, you write entries as if your ideal future has already arrived. Write in the same style as you would in a regular journal. The creating history journal can be used in a variety of instances. Let's say you have an important event coming up and you're feeling nervous and scared. An old, self-defeating behavior would be to worry about the event and imagine all the worst case scenarios so that by the time the event arrives you're a nervous wreck. Even if your worst fantasies don't come true or the event goes wonderfully, you may not be able to enjoy it because you've already worked yourself up to a state of tension and stress. You can use your creating history journal to write about the event as you'd like it to happen. This way you can approach the event with positive expectations and a sense of confidence.

To begin, date the entry, using the date of the event or a later date. For example, if the event is on December 31, write that date, not the date of the day you're writing, at the top of your entry. Then write about the event as if it has already passed and it turned out as you wished.

Kathy was feeling anxious about Mother's Day. It was three weeks away and her mother was coming from out of town for a week-long visit. In the past, there was tension and fighting during visits. Kathy never felt appreciated by her mother and felt her attitude changing for the worse as it came close to time for the visit. Here's a creating history journal entry she wrote:

May 11

My mother just left and we had the best visit ever. I felt less stress than usual because I decided beforehand that I would do my best and let the rest go. It worked! I decided not to have high, unrealistic expectations, so when she showed her appreciation for my gift it felt really good. I'm so glad I decided to do things differently this time. I'm actually looking forward to seeing her again.

Jack wanted to travel and he didn't want to wait until he was in a relationship to do it. Here's the future diary entry he wrote:

September 25

What an incredible day I just had at the Hermitage in St. Petersburg, seeing some of the greatest art in the world. I truly feel blessed to have had the privilege. The architecture, the history—it's all incredible. The cruise that brought us over from the British Isles was one of the most relaxing experiences I've had in a long time. I've been sleeping deeply every night throughout the trip. This has been a time of deep contemplation and spiritual calm for me. To be able to see the hand of God in the sea, the sky, and all around me. There was a time when I would never have had the courage to travel alone. Now look at me! I'm so glad that I faced my fears, one step at a time, and took a chance at living.

Suzanne wanted a trusting, loving marriage with someone of like mind. Here's what she wrote:

Dear Diary,

I can't believe how lucky I've been to find a husband who is such a kind, generous, affectionate man. He really loves me. Actually, luck had nothing to do with it. I'm so glad I had the strength to face my own self-sabotage, go beyond it, and be willing to risk meeting men. My husband is more than I ever could have dreamed of. It's wonderful to have a companion, someone I'm bonded to who is also bonded with me. I love getting phone calls in the middle of the day, someone who is there for me. It's great to be motivated after all the giving I do all day. I love having a friend who enjoys music and opera just like me. I like the direction our relationship is going and the ability we have to communicate. I'm enjoying each day and I'm looking to all of the good times to come.

A creating history journal helps you focus on positive outcomes rather than worrying and focusing on worst case scenarios. Chances are, if you focus on positive, that's what you'll get. Be careful not to get stuck on particular details of how things must go. Simply imagine positive outcomes, positive feelings. You can use the affirmation writing skills you learned in previous chapters to help you. Write about your ideal day in as much vivid detail as possible. Include feelings, sights, sounds, smells, and anything that will make that journal entry come alive for you.

Acting As If Your Goals Are True

Acting as if your goals are true opens your creative mind to the ways and means to actually achieve them. In my workshops, participants engage in a futuristic reunion where each person pretends that it's one year in the future, they've made progress toward their goals, and they're moving in the direction they desire. They pretend like they haven't seen each other for an entire year, so they ask each other things like, "So, what have you been up to?" or "What's new in your life?" The other person has to answer the question as if they already have their ideal life. Many people report that "acting as if" makes them feel better and opens their minds to new ways of seeing things. Several times people have left the workshop realizing they had everything they needed and were ready to take steps toward their goals. By allowing themselves to imagine their goals coming true and realizing nothing horrible would happen as a result, they had the extra push they needed. You can hold your own futuristic reunion with a friend or members of your support group. Here is an example of how it might go:

Ted: Julie, you look really happy. What've you been up to for the past year?

Julie: Well, last year I set a goal to start doing freelance interior design on the side so I could eventually quit my full-time job. It ends up that I got so much work and the pay was so much higher that I had to quit my job! [Acts as if she's currently doing freelance work. Puts out a positive expectancy and has fun.]

Ted: Wow, that's great. Where's your office located?

Julie: Laguna Beach [states her desired business location as if it's already hers].

Ted: We're almost neighbors. I live in Dana Point [states his desired residency].

Julie: What've you been up to this year?

Ted: Well, I finished my book and I got a publisher. My book will be out in six months.

Julie: I'd love to read it when it comes out.

Ted: Why don't we swap phone numbers? I have a bedroom that I've been wanting to redecorate. Maybe you can help me.

Julie: I'd love to.

Notice how the conversation was just like one you would have at a social engagement. However, instead of answering the questions based on today's reality, participants answer them based on desired future reality. Before you do this exercise, take time to think about what you want to be the truth five, ten, or fifteen years from now. Project yourself forward in time, and then have a pretend party or conversation and act as if you are living your dreams right now. Once you plant these ideas in your mind, you open up creative channels that may have previously been blocked.

Task List and Action Plan

Before you go on to the next chapter, take time now to do these activities. They will help you get more out of the rest of this book.

- Make a list of all the positive payoffs for attaining your goals and dreams.

- Daydream about your ideal life as if it were true, imagining how you would feel and how you would act.

- Fold a piece of paper lengthwise. In one column, list your most important goals; in the other column, list the people you know of who have achieved this goal already. Write or call them and ask for advice and guidance.

- Spend ten to fifteen minutes with your eyes closed and repeat one of the following sentences to yourself: "I am clear and receptive. I am ready for my highest good" or "I may not know how this is possible, but it is possible."

- Write a creating history journal entry based on your dream life.

- Get a large piece of sturdy poster board or a photo album with removable pages, as well as a stack of magazines. Cut out pictures and words that symbolize your goals and paste them to the board or in the book. Then put it someplace where you will see it daily.

- Have a futuristic reunion with your friends.

- Each time you notice yourself daydreaming about fear and failure, turn it around and start daydreaming about success.

Seeing Success

1. What do you want to change and why? _____

_____

2. What do you need to do to accomplish this change? _____

_____

3. What are the pros of changing? _____

_____

4. What are your doubts and fears? _____

_____

5. Close your eyes for ten minutes and imagine you have made the changes you desire to make in your life. Imagine this in as much vivid detail as possible. What are

you wearing? Who else is there with you? What is the weather like? What scent surrounds you? After you are finished with this exercise, write your observations below:

_____

_____

_____

_____

6. Close your eyes for ten minutes and imagine yourself doing the necessary footwork toward achieving your goals with ease. Overexaggerate. Imagine yourself floating through the experience effortlessly. Use your affirmation skills to cancel out any negative thoughts that may pop up. After you are finished with this exercise, write your observations: _____

_____

_____

_____

_____

7. Close your eyes for ten minutes and imagine that you are reaping the rewards of change. Allow yourself to be excited about this. After you are finished with this exercise, write your observations: _____

_____

_____

_____

_____

8. Close your eyes for ten minutes and imagine yourself walking through each and every one of your fears. Imagine yourself winning the battle against fear and negativity. After you are finished with this exercise, write your observations: _____

_____

_____

_____

_____

Opening Your Mind

Every time you tell yourself you can't do something or that "it's impossible," it's like a steel door has slammed shut on your creative mind. Writing in your creating history journal can open your mind and get it working on solutions and possibilities. The more often you imagine success the more you exercise your creative muscles and the more efficient the process becomes. As you continue this you may have the following types of experiences:

1. You're reading through the daily paper and suddenly you spot an ad or an article that supports your idea or makes you think of something you otherwise might not have thought of.

2. You have a conversation with someone and suddenly realize that they, or some mutual friend of yours, knows someone who could probably help you make your dream/goal come true.

3. You're looking at the ad section in the newspaper and you see a huge sale on the exact item you need to help you attain your goal.

4. You're driving down the road, spacing out, when suddenly a flash of insight comes to you that may help you achieve your goal.

Although you may not always be in a position to do a futuristic reunion, you can constantly carry yourself like a success, like your dreams have already come true. How would you walk if this were so? How would you carry yourself? How would you interact with others? Really concentrate and try to imagine your ideal life in vivid detail. Feel it deep in your soul. Begin to do this now and as you continue, you may find that you're more likely to attract people, places, things, and situations necessary to do what you desire.

Use the space below to record your creating history journal entry:

_____

_____

_____

_____

_____

_____

_____

_____

_____

_____

8

Success Breeds Success

Knowing What You Want Is the First Step in Getting It

Being successful requires that you know exactly what you want. If you don't sit down and decide what you want in life, life will decide for you. Not having a plan in life is like driving around without a map. You get in the car and turn left because someone tells you to. You turn right because it's convenient, and you keep going until you run out of gas. Not living your dreams is exhausting. It takes a lot of energy to force yourself to be something you're not and to live a life that's unfulfilling.

If you want to get somewhere (rather than driving around aimlessly) dare to be specific. Know where you want to end up in life. Remember also to be flexible in your goals, willing to change your standards, and daring enough to take the road less traveled.

If You Could Do Anything You Wanted, What Would It Be?

When I was twenty-one-years old, I met a man who asked me the question that changed my life: "If you could do anything you wanted to do, what would it be?" The answer for me was easy: "I would go back to school." I had no faith in my ability to accomplish this goal. I was a high school dropout and a drug addict, and to me this meant that I would *never* even be able to complete a college course, let alone get a degree. But this man knew nothing of my doubts and fears, so he drove me to a local community college, dropped me off in the parking lot, pointed to the admissions office, and told me that if I went in the office and filled out the forms, I would be a college student.

I was dumbfounded. I didn't know this man, had never met him before, and never saw him again. But I walked into the admissions office and filled out the forms nonetheless. I turned in the forms and went home. I had no idea when I filled out those forms how I would support myself or how I would pay tuition and buy books. I had no faith that I was smart enough to pass my classes, but once I took that first step, the proceeding steps fell into place. I got a job that was flexible with my school schedule, and I found affordable housing. I learned to access resources such as financial aid and tutoring so I could stay in school and be successful. I excelled in my classes, was given three scholarships, and was placed on the honors list several times. If I had tried to figure out how I was going to do all of this before I did it, I never would have gotten started. Once I got started, everything fell into place.

So, if you could do anything you wanted to do, what would it be? If you can think it, if you can imagine it, if you can dream it, you can make it come true.

Imagine that you had all the resources necessary to reach your dream. Money and time are not obstacles. What would you do? Write your answer on a piece of paper and without judging it or doubting it, ask yourself: "What do I need to do to make this happen?" Take a small step in the direction of your goal. You have nothing to lose by venturing out. You may discover resources you've previously been unaware of. Perhaps by being involved in the process of striving for your goals you will learn more about what you currently have and what you need to make your goal come true.

Success Breeds Success

In order to achieve ongoing success and feel good about it, you need to set attainable goals. Each time you accomplish a goal, you send a message to your brain that you are a success. Remember, what you say is what you get, so it will be to your advantage to focus on success. Doing so gives you the courage, motivation, and stamina necessary to take the next steps to the life you desire. If your focus is on one big goal, each day that you don't accomplish the goal can make you end up feeling like a loser.

Any goal you have can and should be broken down into a step-by-step, manageable plan for success. Focusing on a large goal such as getting out of debt, starting a new business, or mending an estranged relationship can seem overwhelming. The thoughts of such an arduous task can cause you to feel like quitting before you start. Rather than focusing on the big goal and allowing it to mentally overwhelm you, write your goal down. Underneath the goal write all the steps necessary to achieve it. Focus on the steps leading toward your goal. Every time you complete a step, you are closer to your goal. Make your steps small enough so that success is guaranteed.

Look at every goal you have and ask yourself, "What steps do I have to take to accomplish this?" Break every step down to its smallest increment. For example, Joseph wanted to clean out his car. He had been accumulating junk for five years and his car was jam-packed with papers, clothes, books, and trash. The mere thought of cleaning the car made him feel overwhelmed and paralyzed. He listed the steps necessary to accomplish his goal:

1. throw trash away

2. sort through items in car

3. vacuum

4. go to car wash

5. don't add new clutter to car

Even this list seemed overwhelming. He didn't think he could ever clean out all those clothes and books, and he wasn't sure he had room for all of it in his house. He didn't think he could make decisions on what to keep and what to throw away. He reviewed his list again. He felt comfortable with the fifth item on his list, "Don't add new clutter to car." He believed he could accomplish this, but it wouldn't do anything to diminish the pile. The second item on his list, "sort through items in car," seemed impossible. He then broke it down to: "sort through two items in car per day." He felt comfortable with this. Eventually his pile began to shrink, and he felt encouraged and motivated by his success in achieving his smaller goals. He saw a light at the end of the tunnel, and eventually was able to clear five items out a day.

Gradually he progressed to ten items, and within a few months his car was clutter free. It doesn't matter how small your steps are, what matters is that you accomplish them.

Part of becoming successful includes being comfortable with success. Many people sabotage themselves because they aren't used to success. Success feels uncomfortable and foreign, so they sabotage themselves to get back in their comfort zone. Setting small goals and acknowledging them as successes helps you get used to succeeding. Using this method, it's as if success creeps up on you. It's not a drastic change that provokes anxiety, just a slight discomfort that you can overcome. The more experience you have with success, the more comfortable you will be with future successes.

If you have a concept of yourself as a failure, then success probably feels uncomfortable. When the discomfort becomes intense, you may revert to self-sabotaging behaviors in order to feel comfortable again. The greater the success, the greater the chance for self-sabotage. Taking baby steps and focusing on the process of success helps you to gradually become comfortable with success, making you less likely to self-sabotage.

Setting large, unattainable goals also sets you up for failure because you have too long to wait for the encouragement of success. Make your first goal a feasible one that you are willing to work toward. Don't set yourself up for failure by starting with a goal that is overwhelming and fearful. As you become comfortable with success in small goals, your feelings of self-efficacy will build. Next time you start a new project, you will feel stronger because you've already proven your strength and ability. As your self-confidence builds, you can move on to larger goals.

Another way to build your self-confidence is to make a list of all the successes you've had in your life up to this point. List the times you accomplished what you set out to do and review it before taking on a new goal. You may be thinking, "I've never succeeded at anything," but that's a lie. You've succeeded at living this long, so you probably know how to take care of your basic needs. You've succeeded at learning how to read, so you have probably completed some schooling. You've had many successes in your life. Focus on your success and keep a running list that you can refer to later. Be sure to include the successes you've had today, such as getting out of bed, going to work, writing your affirmations, and reading this book. Each and every day you are making progress and moving forward. Don't forget to focus on the baby steps.

Speaking of baby steps, consider how children begin to walk. Long before they can take their first step, there are many preparatory steps (i.e., rolling over, sitting up, scooting on their belly, crawling, exploring in a walker, standing with support, taking steps while holding someone's hand, and finally taking a first independent step). The first steps are followed by many falls. One step, fall, one step, fall, two steps, fall—over and over again until finally they can stand and walk on their own. Each of the preparatory steps is important and necessary. Each one counts. Each day you go to work, each dollar you put in the bank, each time you ask someone for help, each day you attend class—it all counts. Our problems come when impatience takes over and we refuse to focus on the baby steps. Many times in our impatience we force ourselves to move forward. Unless we are mentally ready for success, we're likely to sabotage ourselves and end up further behind than we were to begin with.

Kathleen wasted many years trying to get into shape because every time she made the decision to start a workout program, she went for the gusto. She went from being a couch potato to taking intermediate aerobics. She was a smoker at the time and had some unhealthy eating habits. She got a head rush, sore muscles, and cramps every time she worked out. Who in their right mind would want to maintain a program that made them feel so horrible? Kathleen did the same thing over and over, stop and start, stop and start. She never made any progress.

Finally, she decided that she was only going to exercise three times a week, even when she felt like doing more. She started out with leisurely walks to the beach. As this became routine and enjoyable to her, she upped the pace. Kathleen has been exercising at least three times a week for the past three years. Surely this is better for her body than the harsh treatment she was giving it before. Exercise has become a part of Kathleen's routine.

The impatient/perfectionistic mind may try to suggest that three times a week (or whatever reasonable goals we set for ourselves) is not good enough, but that part of us has not been helpful in moving us toward peaceful fulfillment of our goals. There comes a time when we must tell our perfectionistic/impatient selves, "Thanks for your input," and go about things in a new way.

Henrietta has been trying to clean out her garage for over five years. She can't break free from her all-or-nothing thinking, so she continually dedicates an entire weekend to cleaning her garage. She could probably accomplish a great deal in this weekend. Instead, she looks at the pile of boxes and becomes overwhelmed. She doesn't know where to begin. She puts it off all weekend until finally the weekend is over and her garage is still cluttered. Had she done one box per week she might see some progress, but she believes that one box is not good enough, so her garage stays a cluttered mess.

Setting Small, Manageable Goals

A wise way to attain goals and have ongoing success is to break each goal down into small, manageable steps. Any step you take toward achieving your goal is important because it's moving you closer to your desired end result. Many times we set goals for ourselves with the good intention of changing our lives for the better. But if these goals are so huge and difficult that they will take a long time to accomplish we only end up feeling worse about ourselves in the long run and still won't be any closer to making the changes we desire. For example, if your goal is to graduate from college, don't wait until graduation to feel like a success. Instead, set smaller goals like going to class, passing the next test, turning in the next paper, and eventually finishing the current semester. Without small goals and regular successes, it's easier to get discouraged and give up, or make it to graduation without enjoying the process.

If you're afraid to strive for a better job, start by updating your resume. Since you need a resume to get a new job, updating it is an important step toward your goal. If you've been wanting to start an exercise program but don't feel you have the time, begin with small steps so that you are sure to succeed. Take the stairs instead of the elevator, park your car farther away and walk to your office, walk to the grocery store instead of driving. Once you feel comfortable with this, upgrade your goal to walking longer distances. Increase your exercising from one day a week to two or three. Later you may decide to go even higher. In the meantime, making small, steady increases helps you adjust to exercise and make it a part of your life. It will become a habit and when you don't do it, you'll feel as though something is missing from your life.

If you want to go back to school, start with buying a course catalog, filing out the application, or having your transcripts sent to you. If you want to communicate better with others, start by practicing your communication skills with a supportive friend or spend time each day visualizing yourself as a successful communicator. When you're successful at one portion of your goal, you'll have momentum to strive for the next level. Achieving goals on a step-by-step basis helps you to dip your feet into the success pool a little at a time. As you get comfortable with one level and step in deeper, you adjust accordingly.

If you have trouble completing a task or it seems overwhelming, pick something extremely easy to finish and then applaud yourself for doing so. Many times we feel that small steps aren't worth applause, but remember, each small step adds up and is an important prerequisite to attaining our big goals. Try writing affirmations about patience and visualize yourself achieving your goals. Notice the fears standing in your way and find a way to overcome them.

Everyone feels afraid and overwhelmed at times, but the difference between success and failure is what you do when you are faced with fear and anxiety. If you walk through your fear you'll become stronger and better able to handle future difficulties more effectively. If you avoid the fear, you'll probably feel a temporary relief, but it will be followed by an ever bigger sense of hopelessness and anxiety in the future. You can handle anything that's set in front of you if you break it into small, manageable steps.

If you feel too impatient to allow yourself the smaller goals, remember that this is a self-defeating attitude. If we go full speed ahead into projects proclaiming, "I'm not going to sabotage myself this time," we will likely be unable to meet our unrealistic expectations. Rather than another crash and burn, wouldn't it feel better to have even a tiny bit of success?

Where Are You, and Where Do You Want to Go?

Journals, lists, and graphs can help you see more clearly what needs to be changed and how to change it. Write in your journal about where you are now and where you want to be in the future. Be honest. Matthew wanted to pay off his debt and start an investment account. He kept telling himself he would do it "someday soon." He paid his bills on time but never seemed to make a dent in his debt. He usually only made the minimum monthly payment and he occasionally used his card at the end of the month when all his money was gone. He claimed he didn't have money left over for savings because it all went to bills.

With some reluctance he began to track his spending habits. He also took a close look at his credit card statements. To his dismay he discovered that his minimum monthly payments were 50 percent finance charge and 50 percent capital. At this rate he'd be in debt for ten years. However, to his surprise, he had more disposable income than he realized. He spent twenty dollars a month on video games, one hundred dollars a month on beer, and two hundred dollars a month on eating out. He decided to make changes in his spending habits and apply this extra money to his debt reduction. He also consolidated his bills and shopped around for lower interest rates. He made steady progress and is now over halfway to his goal. Matthew didn't make progress until he honestly assessed his situation. It was uncomfortable to face the truth, but it was necessary for his personal and financial growth.

At the end of this chapter you'll find a graph you can use to determine where you are and where you want to be in various areas of your life. You can use the graph to see which areas of your life need more attention. Let's say your goal is to increase the number of hours you study per day. You'll first want to get an idea of how much you currently study. Before you set a goal, take one week to track how many minutes or hours per day you currently study. Keep an ongoing log of how many hours you intended to study, how many hours you actually studied, and what happened to prevent you from studying the desired number. Once you've figured out how many actual hours you spend studying, you'll want to set small, incremental goals that will eventually lead you to your goal of studying a particular number of hours per day. If you currently study one hour per day but your goal is to study twenty hours a week, you have a gap of thirteen hours to fill. Instead of immediately trying to work yourself up to twenty hours a week, you'll probably have more success with a goal such as one-and-a-half hours per day or ten hours a week. Once you've become accustomed to this increase, you can set a new goal.

Journaling can also help you once you begin working toward your goal. For example, if your goal is two hours of study but you only make it to one hour, write about why you could only make it one hour, how that made you feel, and what the result was. As you continue this process, you'll learn more about how to shift your life, your perceptions, and your goals so that success is assured. For example, if you were too tired to study, you may want to consider two separate one hour blocks of study time. Or maybe the time of day wasn't good for you—perhaps you should study in the morning versus the evening (or vice versa) because you'll be more alert. Maybe the location you've chosen for study is inappropriate and impedes your ability to concentrate. Perhaps instead you should study in the library, outdoors, in a restaurant, or in a room with the door closed. The bottom line is, you can't fail unless you quit. Don't assume that you're never going to be able to change, or that it's too hard. Simply stick with your project until you learn a way to succeed that works for you.

If you continually set goals but seldom accomplish them, don't give up. It may be your plan that needs changing, not you. Continue to strive for your goal, but decrease the size of your steps. When an athlete trains for a track meet, they don't go out and run until they are exhausted and then give up or call themselves a failure. They start small and work themselves up to the challenge. They pace themselves, getting stronger with each practice session.

Most desired behaviors are actually acquired skills that get stronger with practice. As you practice, you'll become better at achieving your desired outcomes. Take a moment now and write about a situation that's easy for you to handle. Perhaps you're a pro at computers or fluent in more than one language. Maybe you're skilled in a trade or handy with crafts. Perhaps you are a musician or artist. Were you always good at these skills, or did you start out feeling uncomfortable and awkward? How many years did you practice before you got good? All change and skill takes time. Everyone has to be a beginner at some point. If you know what you want and are willing to take the steps to get there, you can do whatever you set your mind to.

Mapping Your Goals

One way to break down your goals into manageable steps is to use the goal setting worksheet at the end of this chapter. First write your goal at the top of the worksheet. Below your goal, list the necessary steps you must take to achieve it. If your goal is to get a college degree, there are many things you first must do. You have to sign up for school, then sign up for classes, you must attend the classes, take tests, write papers, and continue these steps each semester until you have attained your goal.

Once you have written your goal and all the steps necessary to achieve it, review each step and consider how long it would take to complete it. Give yourself a time line. Put your goals in one of the following categories: those you can accomplish in the next five years, one year, six months, month, week, or day. You might want to get a set of six markers and write each time frame in a different color. As you do this time line, try to break all goals down to the smallest steps possible. For example, review goals in the one-year category. What can you do on a monthly or weekly basis that will help facilitate completion of your yearly goal? As you break each goal down to its smallest increment, you may be surprised to find that there are several goals you can accomplish right now, such as making phone calls or looking things up at the library. Start where you can and start as soon as possible.

Jim was tired of stressing out every year at tax time. His goal was to be better prepared for taxes the next year. His goals included:

1. save receipts in an organized manner

2. track daily business mileage

3. track expenses

4. track income

5. keep all tax documents in one location

6. pay taxes quarterly to avoid a huge fine

7. contribute two thousand dollars to IRA

8. find out about tax breaks he may be eligible for

9. send taxes by April 1 next year

Here's what his plan of action looked like:

One year goals:

1. pay taxes by April 1 next year

2. have two thousand dollars in IRA for year

3. find out about tax breaks he qualifies for

Six-month goals:

1. learn about a new tax break that might affect me

2. have one thousand dollars in IRA

Three-month goal:

1. pay quarterly taxes

One-month goal:

1. put one hundred and sixty-seven dollars in IRA account

Weekly Goals:

1. get out receipts and put totals in account book

2. buy a file cabinet or make files to keep all tax information in

3. put all tax related information in "Tax inf." file

Daily Goals:

1. get receipts for all expenditures

2. write down all business mileage

3. put receipts in envelope

4. keep track of income

Jim didn't always follow his plan, but he made major improvements and his year was a lot less stressful. By the end of the year he learned a lot about what worked for him. He devised ways to remind himself of his daily goals and he sent his taxes off by April 1 as planned.

Once you take your first step, you've broken out of the comfort zone and you're moving forward. Being involved in the project will probably teach you things you didn't know before you started. Once you're immersed in achieving your new goal, it's likely that the steps you need to follow will unfold naturally. Writing out your goals and taking steps toward achieving them helps you take your goals from the dream or "someday" stage to the reality stage. There are tangible things you can do right now to ensure success. If you stick with your plan of action, you will succeed.

Goal setting is like planting a garden. When you plant a seed, you expect it to someday grow into a plant—and not just any plant, but one that corresponds with the seed you've planted. If you plant a zucchini seed, you expect to one day have a zucchini plant. But first you must plant the seed in fertile soil, water it, and place it in the proper sunlight. If you take the appropriate steps, chances are good that you will one day have a zucchini plant. The same is true with your goals. You should have a firm idea of what your goal is, what you want to grow. Then you should nurture that goal with positive thoughts and action so that one day it will become full-grown. If you take consistent action in a new direction, you will see results. Things may not turn out exactly as you had planned, but sometimes that's good. Sometimes they turn out even better than you'd planned. The most important thing is that you don't give up no matter what.

Flowcharts

A flowchart is a visual and creative way to map your goals. Take out a large piece of paper and draw a circle in the center. Write your goal in the center of the circle (see figure 8.1).

Figure 8.1

Then draw several lines coming out from the circle. On these branches, outline your subgoals and/or the steps you must take to attain your main goal (see figure 8.2). For example, if your goal is to get a master's degree, there are several steps you must take to get accepted and then even more steps you must take to complete your degree. Above is an example of how your flowchart might start. Then, keep branching out until you break your goals down into their smallest increments. When you're finished, you should have one or more goals that you can accomplish within the week (see figure 8.3).

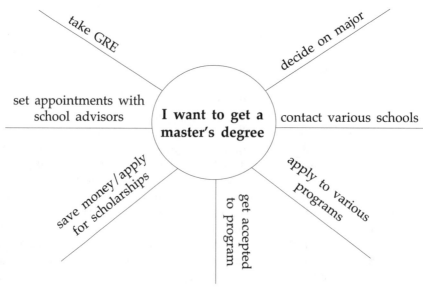

Figure 8.2

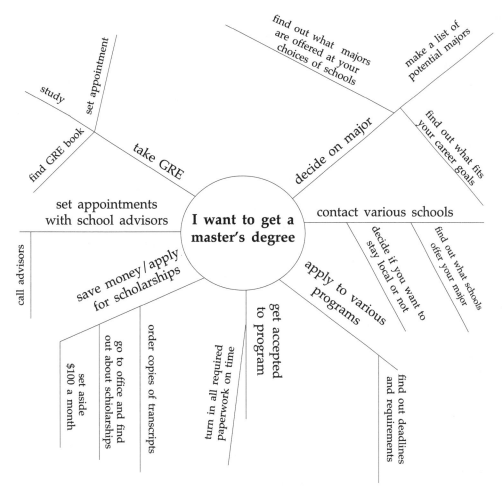

Figure 8.3

After you've mapped out your goals, give yourself a time line. Use a colored pencil and write an anticipated date of accomplishment by each goal. As you accomplish each step, you can cross it off. You might consider mapping this out on a large piece of poster paper or a dry-erase board and placing it someplace where you can see it each day.

Enlisting the Aid of Others

Working with others can help you stay motivated, accountable, and committed to your goals. You might want to consider forming your own goal-setting group. A successful goal-setting group meets regularly to discuss goals, dreams, and aspirations. It's comprised of supportive, like-minded individuals. As you meet with your group regularly, you'll likely become focused and feel accountable. You'll share your goals and your progress. The members will support your progress. The simple act of writing down and then stating your goals makes it much more likely that you'll attain them. You don't have to have the same goals as the people in your group, you simply have to believe in others when they find it difficult to believe in themselves.

A group like this can serve as a form of reward and reinforcement because each time you report your progress, you receive congratulations and praise from your group. You can meet with co-workers, friends, or colleagues. Set a time and day of the week that's convenient for you and commit to each other to keep this weekly appointment. The group should begin with some sort of preamble or ritual to get the focus onto goal setting. After the meeting starts, each member reports his or her progress since the last meeting. Each member reviews their accomplishments and utmost respect is given as members take turns listening to each other. This is not a group for advice giving or nay-saying, but simply offering support. After all progress reports are made, each member then takes turns stating their goals for the upcoming week (or however long until the next meeting), as all members listen attentively and offer support to the person speaking. You may offer this support by using an affirmation such as: "I believe in you and I support you as you move toward your goal."

Task List and Action Plan

Before you go on to the next chapter, take time now to do these activities. They will help you get more out of the rest of this book.

- Have you identified specifically what your goal is? If you could do anything you wanted, what would it be?

- As you work toward your goals, note the things that work for you and don't work for you, as well as why they do/don't work for you.

- Write about a skill or talent you possess. How long did it take you to reach the level you're at now? Can you be patient with yourself as you achieve new goals?

- Fill out the "Where I Am, and Where I Want to Be" graph on the next page, using it as a visual display of the areas of your life that need attention.

- Use the goal setting worksheet that follows to identify your goals and put them on a time line.

- Make a flowchart that outlines your goals.

- As you write your goals, attempt to break them down to the smallest increment possible. If you follow your list of goals diligently, you'll have success.

Where You Are, and Where You Want to Be

	0	1	2	3	4	5	6	7	8	9	10	
Sample	░	░	░	░	░	░						Where You Are
	▓	▓	▓	▓	▓	▓	▓					Where You Want to Be
School												Where You Are
												Where You Want to Be
Friendships												Where You Are
												Where You Want to Be
Family												Where You Are
												Where You Want to Be
Work/Career												Where You Are
												Where You Want to Be
Signif. Other												Where You Are
												Where You Want to Be
Chores												Where You Are
												Where You Want to Be
Helping Others												Where You Are
												Where You Want to Be
Self-Care												Where You Are
												Where You Want to Be
Hobbies												Where You Are
												Where You Want to Be
Rec./Fun time												Where You Are
												Where You Want to Be
Personal Growth												Where You Are
												Where You Want to Be
Exercise/Health												Where You Are
												Where You Want to Be
Debt												Where You Are
												Where You Want to Be
Savings												Where You Are
												Where You Want to Be

Goal Setting Worksheet

My goal is to _____

I want this to be accomplished by: (date) _____

The necessary steps I must take to achieve this goal are:

1. _____
2. _____
3. _____
4. _____
5. _____
6. _____
7. _____
8. _____
9. _____
10. _____
11. _____
12. _____
13. _____
14. _____
15. _____
16. _____
17. _____
18. _____
19. _____
20. _____

Five-year goals:

1. _____
2. _____

3. _____

4. _____

5. _____

Yearly goals:

1. _____

2. _____

3. _____

4. _____

5. _____

Six-month goals:

1. _____

2. _____

3. _____

4. _____

5. _____

Monthly goals:

1. _____

2. _____

3. _____

4. _____

5. _____

Weekly goals:

1. _____

2. _____

3. _____

4. _____

5. _____

Daily goals:

1. _____

2. _____

3. _____

4. _____

5. _____

As you continue to take baby steps toward your goals, it'll become easier and easier and the following steps will unfold naturally. There are tangible things you can do right now to ensure success. If you stick with your plan of action, you will succeed.

9

Acknowledging Your Strengths and Successes

It's a good idea to write your goals and values at the beginning of each year. Every day write down progress you've made toward achieving that goal (i.e., called a business associate, visualized success, wrote affirmations, went to the library, read a book about your area of interest, talked to someone about your goal, met with your goal group, went to the gym, didn't use your credit cards, didn't smoke, etc.). You don't have to wait for a monumental change to take place before you consider it a success.

Most of us have a tendency to downplay and/or forget our successes. Writing your successes down can help you keep your focus on the positive events in your life. Any change you make—no matter how small—is a success. Little successes add up to make bigger successes. As you journal, keep track of the chain of events that led to your success so you can repeat it in the future. Sometimes you can do things to make success more likely, such as getting enough sleep, meditating, and eating healthy foods. Making note of your success strategies is a good idea so you can repeat them in the future.

When attempting to change, it's likely that your self-defeating inner voice will say, "You're not doing good enough," or "It's not worth it to try." You may find yourself focusing on all of your failures and setbacks while forgetting the progress you've made. It's at times like these that your success lists will be invaluable. When you are feeling down or wanting to quit, you can refer back to them for a boost and prove to yourself that you have changed. Sometimes change happens slowly, but if you continue on your new path you will progress. It's natural to have setbacks, but remember, you won't fail unless you quit. Setbacks are not failures, they're learning experiences. Use them to teach you what needs to be changed.

Tracking Techniques

There are several ways to keep track of your success. One is to simply write them down in a notebook every day. Keep this notebook in a special place and set aside five minutes at night to write in it. You don't have to write anything elaborate. You could just write short sentences or phrases (i.e., went to the gym, wrote one page of affirmations, called ten sales leads). You may want to keep your written goals and list of accomplishments all in one place, perhaps in a calendar or notebook. Find a way that is convenient for you so you can get in the habit of writing down and focusing on your success daily.

Another way to track your progress is to write your successes in a blank check register. Then write imaginary payments or deposits for each success. "Pay" yourself in your check register at the end of each day for a job well done. Once you get a certain amount, you can take yourself someplace special or buy yourself a gift. Use your list of necessary actions from your goal setting worksheet and assign rewards for each subgoal. For example, if you are a salesperson and you want to make more money in sales, there are several steps you might take, such as making cold calls, calling back old clients, sending a mailer, coming up with promotional ideas, setting up a booth at a convention, or distributing fliers.

Now that you have your list, review it and note which tasks are easy for you to complete and which are difficult. Assign a dollar amount to each action or behavior on your list, paying yourself more money for difficult things and less money for the easy things. If cold calls are difficult for you but updating old accounts is easy, you might pay yourself one thousand for cold calls and only one hundred for updating old accounts. Make a deal with yourself that every time you make a cold call, you get to deposit in your imaginary bank account. Each time you "earn" a particular amount, such as ten thousand dollars, you can treat yourself to something you enjoy. The more difficult something is for you, the higher and more frequent the reward should be. As the new behavior becomes more automatic, you should pay yourself less and less. Eventually the reward should be the satisfaction of accomplishment.

You can also use a point system to track your successes. For example, each time you do things in a new and positive way, you could track it giving yourself a point for each positive behavior. Or maybe you could do the same for each hour or day that passes that you don't engage in negative behavior. For example, you could give yourself a point for each hour you don't smoke or overeat. Then, once you get a certain number of points, you can reward yourself with something positive. You may want to award yourself a high number of points for difficult behaviors and lower amounts for easier behaviors. Then once you've reached a predetermined number of points, give yourself a reward.

Using tokens is another method of record keeping. You could put tokens, marbles, or small pieces of paper in your right-hand pocket. Then each time you do things a new way, transfer a token to your left-hand pocket. At the end of the day, count your tokens and reward yourself accordingly. The idea behind this is to design a project that's fun and motivating. This reward system helps you focus on winning and helps you forget about fear and taking risks. Whatever reward you choose, it should be motivating enough that you want it more than you want to engage in old behavior, and it should be attainable. Don't wait to make one thousand points before you reward yourself, and don't set your reward so high that you won't be able to easily attain it.

Rewarding Your Success

There are many ways to reward yourself, but what's important is that the rewards are positive, immediate, and attainable. When Clara was attempting to cut her caffeine intake, she paid herself one dollar in real money for every day she didn't drink coffee, black tea, or soda. When she accumulated seven dollars, she went to a clothing store in town where everything was seven dollars and bought herself something new. This reward was affordable, feasible, and fun for Clara.

Be sure to make your reward feasible. Make it something affordable and something that you'll be motivated to work toward. A friend of mine told me that she decided to quit smoking and used a Hawaiian vacation as her reward. She saved all of her cigarette money in a can decorated with pictures of Hawaii and within a year was able to take the vacation of her dreams. Every day she didn't smoke, she imagined her trip to Hawaii. In the end, she got two rewards: better health and a tropical vacation. Below is a list of reward ideas. Use these ideas to help design your own list of things you love to do so you can use them as rewards in the future.

- take a bubble bath
- go to a movie or a play
- take a day off work and have fun
- go out dancing

- go to the beach
- listen to your favorite music
- eat your favorite food
- write in your journal
- spend money
- pamper yourself
- get out of debt
- lie in the sun
- doodle
- fly a kite
- rollerskate or rollerblade
- paint
- sing
- go somewhere and people watch
- go to a concert
- play with pets
- dance
- go to lunch with a friend
- do crossword puzzles
- talk on the phone
- light candles
- get a massage
- take a sauna or a steam bath

- spend time at a favorite hobby
- watch TV
- spend time in the garden
- play a game
- spend extra time with a friend
- read your favorite book or magazine
- go on a vacation
- wear new clothes
- play a sport
- buy fresh flowers
- go sailing
- do crafts
- go sightseeing
- go to a spectator sport
- photography
- play with children
- go on a picnic
- call someone long distance
- play on the computer
- go to the museum
- listen to the radio
- buy books
- get dressed up

Another fun reward is to write yourself a congratulations letter for a job well done and then send it to yourself. It could say something like, "I'm so proud of you for the hard work you've put into changing, I really notice a difference in you. Keep up the good work—you deserve it!" When you send the letter to yourself in the mail, you get two added benefits. One is that you never know when it's going to come back to you, and you may get it at a time when you're feeling down and need it most. The other benefit is that going to the mailbox, opening the envelope, and reading the letter makes it seem more official, like a real letter. Reading the letter can boost your self-esteem as much or more than if you received the letter from someone else. One of the benefits of writing your own support letter is that it will say exactly what you want to hear. Take that into consideration and write the most elaborately supportive letter you can imagine.

If you have a reminder service on your voicemail or on your computer, you can send yourself a positive statement. Program your phone to call you at a certain time of day to remind you of this positive statement or use a computerized reminder system to send yourself messages. You can also call your own answering machine or voicemail and leave positive messages of congratulations to hear when you get home or when you check your messages. Perhaps you can buy yourself flowers and put them in a prominent place where you will see them often. Make out your own card that says, "Congratulations," "Keep up the good work," or "I love you." If you act like you deserve good things and you treat yourself well, eventually you'll believe it.

If you belong to a support group of any kind, you can exchange positive feedback with each other. To begin, get a piece of paper and put your name at the top of it. Then, each person passes their paper to the left while everyone takes turns writing positive things about each other. As the papers get passed around, everyone will have a chance to compliment all the members of the group. When everyone is finished, you will be given a sheet filled with positive comments about you. You'll have had the opportunity to give compliments to all the people in your group. Each person gets to keep their own list to take home so they can refer back to it later. You may not have been given the support you craved as a child, but you can give yourself support today. You can be your own good parent.

Being Yourself Makes It Easier to Succeed

Robert Louis Stevenson once said that, success is "To be what we are and to become what we are capable of becoming." You have a unique role to play in this life. No one else possesses the exact set of skills and life experiences you do. No one else can fill the shoes you were meant to fill, no one else can do as good a job at being you as you can. If you allow yourself to be "you," there's no way you can fail. Being yourself is natural. Chances are, part of your self-sabotage stems from trying to be something you're not. It's hard to do something uninteresting. It's hard to pretend, fake, or force yourself into a role you're not suited for.

On one of my trips across the desert from Los Angeles to Phoenix, I marveled at the many cacti that sprinkled the dry, hot expanse of land on either side of the highway. I reflected on how effortlessly they grew with no help from a gardener. As the sun set, I marveled at the beautiful colors that spread across the sky. I reflected on how effortlessly nature "does its thing" and realized that when we are one with our own nature, our lives also become effortless. It's when we try to be something that we're not that trouble and hard work is introduced. The cacti that grew unattended would not fare so well if they were uprooted and shipped to Minnesota, because they're not meant to grow in Minnesota. And so it is with us.

We have certain areas that we grow in naturally. Some of us are automatically good at a particular field or subject. Some are excellent communicators or great with children. Some have a knack for arts and crafts, others a passion for electronics and computing. When we work in these areas, we succeed with ease, yet when we transplant ourselves to other areas, we wilt. This isn't to say we shouldn't try to expand, but we should acknowledge and work with our innate talents. They were given to us for a reason and we shouldn't ignore them.

Goals based on your true desires and talents will be easier to succeed at. You may feel like a failure because you haven't succeeded at the goals you've set for yourself in life, but it's possible that you were trying to attain the wrong goal. Think of some of the goals you failed to accomplish and ask yourself how important they were to you. Were they deep, yearning goals that you've held since childhood? Were they in line with your values and interests? Did you really want to attain those goals or did you strive for them because you thought you should?

Nancy was a miserable failure at working nine to five, Monday through Friday. She attempted desk jobs repeatedly because she thought that was the "responsible, adult" thing to do. She said, "I'm a complete airhead before noon. I can't spell or file properly in the morning and I'm crabby. I was lazy at desk jobs. I was so overwhelmed with boredom that I could barely keep my eyes open. I made stupid mistakes. I felt like a failure. When I finally started to do work that I loved and was able to set my own schedule, my talents began to shine. When I'm doing work I love I can juggle three things at once and get them all done correctly and on time. I can take a job that would take some people five hours to complete and do it in one."

When Nancy decided to be true to herself it meant spending many years juggling full-time school, full-time work, and a part-time web-design career. She said, "It was easy because I loved what I did. When I worked a nine-to-five desk job, it was all I could do to get through the day so I could go home, watch TV, and go to bed so I could get up early the next day. Now I have plenty of energy to live my life." As your goals become more in tune with your true self, you will experience higher levels of success in your life with lower levels of effort and strain. Being yourself is not hard to do. Being natural comes naturally. Perhaps the reason you've had to struggle for success is because you've been fighting against your true nature. Even when you do attain success while being "unnatural," you have to struggle to keep it. Are you truly successful if your life is riddled with struggle and stress? Can you really ever enjoy life as long as you're trying to please others?

Who Am I?

What if you don't even know who you are? This is a common concern. Some of us have grown so accustomed to listening to other people's advice in favor of our own that we have no idea who we are or what we really want to do. How can you take true risks if you don't even know what's important to you, what you think, or how you feel? Start by answering the following questions honestly. Try not to answer them the way you think you "should." Don't edit your answers in your mind before you get a chance to respond. There's no right or wrong answer. These same questions are asked in the worksheet at the end of the chapter for your convenience.

- If I had abundant money and time, and I could do anything in the world, I would . . .

- If I could change one thing about this world it would be . . .

- The most important thing I own is . . .

- I love to . . .

- I feel most alive when . . .

- I love to give . . .

- Throughout the years, the consistent quality or attribute that other people have appreciated in me is . . .

- Thinking of three special people currently in my life, I think they'd say the following things are unique and special about me . . .

The answers to these questions will give you a clue as to what's important to you and can be used to help you formulate life goals. Daily meditation and journaling are also excellent tools to use in getting to know yourself.

In your journal, reflect on the following thoughts, adapted from *Fulfill Your Soul's Purpose* by Naomi Stephan.

1. What are you passionate about?

2. What gives you energy?

3. Pay attention to your body's aches and pains. Dr. Naomi Stephan writes, "When you fail to respond to your inner wisdom, you'll feel specific emotional and physical reactions resulting from that neglect."

4. Fear may also be an indicator that you're running away from what you love. Write out your fears. What are they trying to tell you?

5. Take note of activities that offer rewards in your life.

6. Write about the heroes you admired as a child look for clues as to what you value and admire.

7. Consider your favorite hobbies or books you read as a child. Do you find any common themes?

Try the following exercise as a way to get in touch with who you are. Take a few deep breaths to calm down, then imagine yourself sitting in a comfortable, familiar, safe place. Think of a person or entity that you trust. Imagine this person or entity sitting next to you. You can tell this being anything and it will love you unconditionally. You don't need to wear masks or put on a facade in the presence of this special person or entity. Time spent in this presence is carefree and natural. Imagine yourself reverting to a childlike, carefree individual and communicating that free-spiritedness with this trusting soul. Be yourself. Practice this ritual daily and allow yourself to be okay with this freedom. As time passes, you will find yourself better able to be free-spirited around others. Allow yourself to relish in the fun of it all.

Developing a relationship with yourself is similar to developing a relationship with someone else—it takes time and open communication, it takes asking questions and listening for answers. It requires spending time focusing on your needs. These are the things you need to do with yourself if you really want to know yourself. Write out lists of things that are important to you, things you value, things you enjoy. Go places that are special to you, spend time in nature, take yourself shopping or to the movies, buy yourself flowers. Sit quietly in a room with yourself and let yourself be whatever you are. If you feel like crying, cry. If you feel like laughing, laugh. Be the real you, the person you would allow yourself to be in the presence of someone you deeply trust. Let go of all "shoulds" and put aside the masks for a while. Be the you that has been yearning to express itself since day one, that innocent, childlike self that your uniqueness rejoices in.

Chances are you've had a lot of negative ideas piled on you that lead you to believe that being yourself just isn't good enough. You don't have to learn to be yourself, you have to *unlearn* any idea that it's not okay to be yourself—then you'll experience a splendid beauty.

Some of the techniques and exercises outlined in this book might intimidate you. Perhaps your instinct is to pass them up and get back to them later. Break through any fear or resistance you have and do the exercises. Regardless of the direct or immediate benefits you gain from the exercises themselves, taking time to do them sets a cycle in motion. It breaks you out of your comfort zone and gets you in the process of change. You have nothing to lose by doing them. Forgo the voice that says, "I don't need to," or "I've already done stuff like this before and it didn't work." These exercises don't generally work immediately, like magic. They have a cumulative effect. The first time you do them may not seem to make any difference, but it does. Each successive time you try these exercises you'll notice even greater benefit. It does work but it takes time.

What Do I Want?

At the end of the chapter you will find a "create the life you want" questionnaire. This questionnaire can help you decide what you want from life. It is a lengthy questionnaire that will probably take at least an hour to complete. If you really want to know yourself and live your own life, it will take time, maybe a lifetime, but it's better than the alternative of feeling dead, helpless or depressed, of waking up one day and wondering where the past twenty years of your life have gone. When you fill out the questionnaire you'll be asked to identify the areas most important in your life right now and what steps you can take to move closer to where you want your life to be. You might realize that you already have what you want in some areas of life. You might also find that you already have what you need to achieve some of your unmet goals. Make a list of the things that you do have now. This list can include tangible items such as money, a computer, a fax machine, or a telephone or it can include intangible things such as desire, determination, and willingness.

Many times we fail to acknowledge that we have resources available to us right now that will move us in the direction of our goals. We focus on what we need and want, but not what we already have. Often times if we take steps toward our goals we become aware of what needs to be done simply because we're in the flow of taking action. Even if we make mistakes, we learn from them. This experience will lay an invaluable groundwork for the goals to come.

Sometimes our goals and dreams are unattainable. However, when reviewed closely we may find that they point to a missing link in our lives. You might say you want to win a million dollars, but why? You say you want a new relationship, but why? What's under the goal or desire? What does a million dollars or a new relationship symbolize to you? What will attaining this goal bring to your life? Many times if we look closely we see that we want a million dollars because it symbolizes security or independence or we think that if we had a million dollars, we'd have more friends or get to travel more or be free from debt.

What we fail to see is that there are ways to bring love, security, and independence into our life without having to win a million dollars. Some of us will have specific goals and dreams that will not come true in this lifetime. For example, if you are forty and you want to play pro ball, you probably won't see that as a reality, but you can probably have what that goal symbolizes. If you want to be a professional athlete so that people will adore you or pay attention to you or because you want fame, find out how you can get recognition doing something you enjoy that is attainable now. What's underneath your goals? Chances are, under your goals is where you will find your values. You can live your life in accordance with your values despite your age, financial status, or educational level.

Juan said he wanted to have $100,000 in the bank so he could feel sure his children had a "good life" when they were older. He wanted them to have some money for college. He worked two jobs so he could accomplish his goal. He wanted to hurry up and accomplish it so he could quit one of his jobs and spend more time with his family. One day his daughter got upset with him. She was angry that he didn't spend more time at home. Juan was angry that she didn't appreciate all his hard work. What Juan didn't realize is that his idea of a good life was different from that of his children.

He didn't have to work two jobs to give his children a good life. What they really wanted was to see their dad more often. Juan realized that there were other ways to provide for the kids' education, such as scholarships and loans. When the family discussed the matter together they came up with new ideas such as after-school jobs and cutting current expenses. Juan spent time helping the kids with their homework so they could do better in school. They were able to come up with a plan that suited all their needs.

The True Self and Self-Esteem

Many people identify low self-esteem as the cause of their self-defeating behavior. Having esteem for your true self means accepting and loving your hidden values, your innermost thoughts and feelings, your unexposed talent, and your vulnerabilities. It includes your likes, dislikes, strengths, and weaknesses—*all* of you.

Many of us have lost touch with our true selves. We become wrapped up in doing things the way we think we "should." Some of us have given up our dreams in favor of the security of a weekly paycheck or to avoid rejection from our friends and family. As long as we are living by the rules of others, we are esteeming them, not ourselves. We'll never know true self-esteem or complete success while living out the wishes of others. We might be able to attain the trappings of success, but we can never feel as excited and happy about life as we can when we're true to ourselves.

You may be thinking, "I already know what my true self is like. I'm selfish, greedy, insecure, perfectionistic, and dishonest. If I let myself go, my life will really be screwed up. The reason I read books like this is to change myself." The purpose of this book is to uncover the true you. The true you is not selfish, greedy, insecure, perfectionistic, and dishonest. Those attitudes are a reaction or defense, not an authentic personality style. This book is designed to help you stop the negative behaviors and beliefs that block you from expressing your true self.

You might act selfish, impatient, needy and greedy, and maybe that's not so bad. Perhaps these actions have helped you to feel comfortable and safe. Maybe you needed them to help you deal with harmful, unpredictable, and chaotic situations in the past. Maybe there's a time and a place for all of your defects. Maybe instead of trying to change your entire personality you need to find a place where your personality will be put to good use. Or perhaps your energy needs to be redirected.

Rebellion is a behavior that's often seen as negative. As children we learn to respect our elders and not to disobey. Yet if it weren't for rebels, we wouldn't have had a civil rights movement. If it weren't for "pushy" and "demanding" women, we wouldn't have ever started a women's movement. Women still might not have the right to vote and domestic violence would still be considered the husband's right, not a violent crime. If it weren't for perfectionistic types, where would science and technology be today? Do you want a computer designed by a perfectionist or an easygoing, free-flowing type? If it weren't for the artists and visionaries—who are often labeled "weirdoes" and accused of living in their own world—where would we be?

There is a place for all personality types and all talents. Even traits we've assumed to be entirely negative, such as impatience, have some value and can be used constructively. For example, impatience can be used to get things done. Many of us have a talent that comes so naturally to us that we don't even realize it's a talent. Beatrice always wanted to be like her friend Lucy, an actress. One day Lucy told Beatrice, "But you can say and write things that make perfect sense. I have to struggle to get my words out." Beatrice realized that words had been her talent for many years. She won all the spelling bees in elementary school and was really good at talking her way out of trouble. She did well in English and writing classes, kept a journal for many years, and was an avid reader. When she lived in a small town, her favorite day of the week was when the bookmobile would come so she could get some new books. Beatrice said, "When I think about it, it makes perfect sense that I'd be a writer and speaker, but I've spent most of my life wishing I could be someone else instead of valuing my own talents." Once she recognized her innate talents, she began to succeed like never before. She's good at what she does, and she enjoys herself tremendously.

In one of my workshops I had each person write a short description of themselves on an index card. I told them to write what a good friend would write. Then, I chose a card a random and, without disclosing the person's name, I wrote the characteristics on the board. As a group we came up with a list of things this anonymous person was probably good at. Many people are surprised to find that the traits they think are ho-hum or negative are viewed very positively by other workshop participants. For example, one woman wrote that she's sensitive, organized, detail oriented, conservative, and an impulsive decision maker. As a group we brainstormed times and places that these traits might be useful. We decided that she would make a good manager because she's sensitive to the needs of others and detail oriented. We further discussed how impulsive decision making is sometimes necessary and preferable to mulling over a decision. This woman had never stopped to consider that her traits were positive.

She, like many of us, had been told things like, "You're so sensitive," in a judgmental tone that implied, "Why do you take everything so personal? Why can't you just lighten up? You just can't take a joke." Because others in her life condemned, ridiculed, or belittled her sensitivity, she began trying to hide it. She tried to be more tough. She never thought to embrace the positive aspects of being sensitive. As the workshop continued we discussed how horrible it would be if no one was sensitive, if everyone was hard and callous. We discussed how important and valuable it is to have sensitive people in the world. Reflect on some of your own personality traits and how you perceive them. Chances are, you've been your harshest critic. Now it's time to see your skills and talents in a new light.

You may want to try this exercise with a friend or support group. Others will be able to give you a more objective view of your personality. Another thing you can do with a large group is randomly choose a card and see if you can think of any famous or important people who fit the same description as the one on the card. In the following list, which famous people do you think these descriptions could describe?

argumentative	adventurous
opinionated	outdoorsy
happy	spontaneous
pleasant	able to succeed
cheerful	generous (to a fault)
loyal	flexible
different from the crowd (especially in social/political beliefs)	able to change at a moment's notice

While most people admire traits like perseverance, dedication, strong will, and rebellion in others, they tend to criticize these traits or try to change them when they come up in themselves. Today is the day for you to begin admiring yourself. I know, I know—it feels selfish to admire yourself, it seems conceited. But really you're being selfish by keeping your gifts and talents hidden. The world needs them! You're not helping anyone by staying in your shell. You were given your gifts for a reason, and now it's time to put them to use.

When Guglielmo Marconi first discussed his concept of wireless radio transmission, people thought he was crazy. Family members wanted to have him committed. Thanks to a "crazy" person we have radio. As you take risks and share your ideas, some people may think you're weird. Just because someone thinks that, doesn't mean that it's true. Some people will call new ideas crazy, weird, and impossible simply because change is threatening. When people see you breaking through barriers, it can make them uncomfortable.

But you don't have to stay stuck just to fit in with everyone else. You can move forward with or without the support of your current social circle. Some people might just decide to get up and follow you. Others might disown you. This is a part of risk-taking. As you continue to stay true to yourself, chances are you'll meet new people who will support the new you.

Looking for Love in All the Wrong Places

Many of us learned in childhood that in order to be loved and accepted, we need to behave a certain way. We may have abandoned our childlike enthusiasm and stopped taking risks in favor of gaining approval. John Stevens says: "If I calculate and put on phony behavior in order to please you, you may love my *behavior*, but you cannot love *me*, because I have hidden my real existence behind this artificial behavior. Even when you love in response to my phony behavior, I cannot really receive your love. It is poisoned by my knowledge that the love is for the image I have created, not for me. I also have to be continually on guard to be sure that I maintain my image so that your love does not disappear. Since I have shut myself off from your love in this way, I will feel more lonely and unloved, and try even more desperately to manipulate myself and you in order to get this love" (Stevens 1971).

True love can never be attained if one is acting a part and being fake. The behavior you have engaged in and worked so long and hard to perfect is useless in helping you to attain the very thing you want so desperately. The people who matter, those who truly love you, will know that you've been faking it all along. They are likely wondering when you're going to drop the act and just be yourself. Taking risks benefits you in many ways, including attaining true love.

Being True to Yourself Isn't Selfish

Some people sabotage their success or refrain from attaining a goal because they've learned that success is selfish or that poverty is a virtue. Nothing could be further from the truth. Imagine how your life would improve if you were doing the work you love to do, traveling in places you always wanted to go to, and spending time with people you love. How do you suppose you would feel if you were living your dreams? How would you interact with others?

Don't feel guilty about achieving your goals and taking risks. When you act on your inner desires it will only make your own and other people's lives better. What do you think would be more likely to benefit society, a world of miserable people or a world of happy people? Can you imagine how much better the world would be if everyone was feeling happy, joyous, free, and fulfilled? When you are happy and fulfilled, you'll have a positive influence on people around you. Of course, knowing this may not make your work any easier. Change is always uncomfortable in the beginning, but it gets easier with time and is worth the effort. The only way out of the discomfort is through it.

Task List and Action Plan

Before you go on to the next chapter, take time now to do these activities. They will help you get more out of the rest of this book.

- Choose a record-keeping technique that will work for you and use it daily (point system, success list, tokens, checkbook register).

- Write a list of rewards that you'll use to reward your new behaviors.

- Write a list of your qualities, negative and positive. See how you can channel your energy to productive, life-enhancing projects.

- Esteem yourself. Listen to your inner voice, follow your own advice. Acknowledge your innate talents.

- Write a list of qualities you admire in others. See which qualities match up to the ones on your own list.

- Take time every day to either meditate, do something you love, or spend time journaling.

- Fill out the "create the life you want" questionnaire and formulate goals based on your writing.

- Make a list of all the things you have to attain your goals.

- Fill out the "know yourself, love yourself" questionnaire at the end of this chapter.

- After you define your goals, complete the following sentence: "I want this goal because . . ." See if you can have what the goal symbolizes now, without having to wait for the goal to come true. Brainstorm new possibilities.

Success Rewards

Write a list of goals you want to accomplish in the first column. In the second column, assign reward points for each task.

Goals	Point Value

In the first column, write a list of things you like to do and that would seem rewarding to you. Based on the feasibility and cost of these rewards, how many points do you need to earn for each reward? Write the amount in the second column.

Rewards	Point Value

Success Journal

In the success column, write any step you took toward your goal.

Date	Success	Points Earned	Daily Total

Know Yourself, Love Yourself

1. Three things that are most important to me are: _____

   _____

   _____

2. If I could change one thing in this world it would be: _____

   _____

   _____

3. The most important thing I own is: _____

   _____

   _____

4. What I really want to do more than anything is: _____

   _____

   _____

5. If I had abundant money and abundant time and could do anything in the world, I would _____

   _____

   _____

6. What do you love to do? _____

   _____

   _____

7. What do you love to give? _____

   _____

   _____

8. What brings you joy? _____

   _____

   _____

9. Through the years, what has been a consistent quality or attribute that other people have appreciated in you? _____

   _____

   _____

10. Think of three people who know you well. What would each of them say is unique or special about you?

    i. _____

    ii. _____

    iii. _____

Create the Life You Want

1. If you knew it were impossible to fail and money wasn't an object, what would you do right now?

_____

_____

2. Would you travel? If so, where to?

_____

_____

3. What would you buy? A home? A car? Stocks and bonds?

_____

_____

4. What would your career include? Would it be fast-paced? Would it include travel? Would you work at a desk, on the road, or not at all? How many hours a week would you work?

_____

_____

5. Would you go to school? Would you go part-time or full-time? What would you major in? Which school would you go to?

_____

_____

6. What would your family life be like? Would you spend more or less time with your family? Would you be closer to your family or more independent?

_____

_____

7. What would your health be like? Would you cut your fat intake? Would you become a vegetarian? Would you exercise? If so, how often? What type of shape would you like your body to be in? What types of exercise would you do? Do you like sports, dancing, aerobics, bike riding, walking, or another kind of exercise the best?

_____

_____

8. What would your spiritual life be like? Would you go to church weekly or read your religious text? Would you pray or meditate? Would you be religious or spiritual? Do you prefer Eastern philosophy or Western religion?

_____

_____

9. Where would you live? On a farm? At the beach? In the mountains? In a house? In an apartment? What country would you live in? What state? What city?

_____

_____

10. What would your personality be like? Would you be more outgoing? Or would you spend more time alone? Would you give more or would you learn to be more selfish? Would you laugh more? Would you cry more?

_____

_____

11. What kind of friends would you have? Rich, poor, influential, kind, giving, loving, supportive, distant, superficial, aloof, people with a good sense of humor, quiet people, loud people, hard workers, high achievers, educated, uneducated, affectionate, earthy?

_____

_____

12. How would you feel most of the time? Aggressive, arrogant, bashful, blissful, bored, confident, curious, determined, ecstatic, happy, interested, joyful, lovestruck, optimistic, satisfied, smug, thoughtful?

_____

_____

13. How would you look/dress? Professional, athletic, casual, comfortable, classy, fashionable?

_____

_____

14. What hobbies would you engage in? Gardening, stamp collecting, reading, scuba diving, swimming, surfing, rollerblading, water skiing, snow skiing, kite flying, crocheting, knitting, cross-stitching, sewing, parasailing, bird watching, collecting knickknacks or antiques, garage-sale shopping?

_____

_____

15. What would your love life be like? Romantic, passionate, predictable, spontaneous, steady?

_____

_____

16. What would your lover be like? Kind, loving, compassionate, hard working, good at parenting, humble, romantic, good sense of humor, attractive, successful, feminine, masculine?

_____

_____

17. Now, go back over your list and put a star next to those that are most important to you. Write a paragraph or two about how your life will improve as a result of doing these things.

_____

_____

_____

_____

_____

18. What do you have already to achieve your goals?

_____

_____

19. Use the goal-setting worksheet to formulate a plan for making these goals come true.

_____

_____

10

Stop Settling and Start Living

Helen Keller once said, "Life is either a daring adventure or nothing at all." One thing we can all be sure of is that our life will end some day. We have no idea when or how, but it will happen. With this in mind, each new day is a gift, filled with opportunities. How will you use your gift? Will you complain that it isn't enough? Will you waste it? Will you use it to its full potential?

Most people don't like to think about death, but it can help motivate us to live our lives to the fullest. If you were told that you only had a short time to live, what do you suppose would be important to you at that moment? Would it matter that you have a lot of money in the bank? Would you feel satisfied with how you've spent your days? What would you regret? What would you be proud of? As you live out the rest of this day, why not live it as if it were your last? Live it so you can feel satisfied that you spent it well.

Now imagine your funeral. What would you like people to say about you? What type of legacy will you leave behind? Will people care that you made wise investments or paid your bills on time, or will they remember your warmth and caring? Will they talk about how you lived your life with gusto or will they be sad that they never felt close to you? Why not live today so that you can move toward the person you want to become?

Only the Person Who Risks Is Free

Each of us has a special gift that yearns to be expressed. When you put up a false front, you're suppressing emotions, thoughts, and feelings that are a natural part of you, and this takes a lot of extra energy. This suppressed energy can cause illness and speed the aging process. It simply wears you out. When you live fully, acknowledge and act on your inner desires, and take risks, you have more energy. You lose track of time, smile more, and enjoy life more because you're actually involved in it personally versus acting out someone else's script.

Let go of rules and yesterday's ideas, and dare to live in the now, and you will be free. Any action you take in life involves risk—whether you let your emotions out or suppress them, whether you share your dreams or keep them tucked away. Love and hope are risks. There's always a chance of being seen as foolish or being rejected. However, taking risks can allow you to live fully and have more of what you want from life.

The Safe Way: Avoiding Risks

Risk-taking is the difference between existing and living. Existing is mere survival, breathing in and out, sleeping and eating, going about life day after day without experiencing excitement or enthusiasm about anything. Living is thriving and being excited about life. It's noticing the tiny details that make life grand and being grateful, joyful, and awed by the beauty of it all. Living entails taking risks. A true risk is being willing to say, "This is who I truly am, this is what I hold deep in my heart, and I am willing to show myself to the world." In our society risk-taking is sometimes likened to daredevil or scandalous activities. But taking risks solely so that people will think you're brave is not really a risk. A true risk entails acting on your innermost dreams and desires. Perhaps you've felt a calling to do something different with your life. Maybe you have unique ideas about developing a product or a program. Perhaps you have creative ideas that never make it to fruition. These ideas and inspirations come from deep within and will probably never go away. They hold the key to your happiness and contentment with life. Take a risk and listen to your inner voice rather than doing what you think you should do. Move from the safe mode into the mode of living fully.

Things That Keep Us Stuck

Our "safe" mode or comfort zone often dictates what types of experiences we allow ourselves to have. There are many factors that comprise our comfort zone, such as our socioeconomic status, the family we grew up in, our friends, our neighborhood or surroundings, the jobs we've held, the people we've worked with, the amount of life experience we've had, the era we live in, and the resources we've had available to us. Most of us have one or more ideas that hold us back from our true potential, and many times these ideas were born years ago and nurtured without question.

To be human is to have limited thinking. Our limited thinking leads to limited life experience, because we only try to do what we believe we can. Our limited experiences then create our limited ideas about "how life is." Now's the time to bring some of these beliefs into the light where they can be examined more clearly. Once we've exposed our true beliefs and their origins, we can decide if we want to keep them or throw them away. As we become more aware of these beliefs, we may realize that they are old and out of date.

A friend of mine once told me a story that illustrates the results of limited thinking in a humorous way. A mother and daughter are in the kitchen cooking an Easter ham as grandma looks on. The daughter asks her mother, "Mommy, why do you cut the ends off the ham before you put it in the pan?" The mother pauses and says, "I don't know, that's the way grandma always did it." So they turn to ask grandma and she says, "I don't know, that's the way my mom always did it." So, they call great-grandma in Ohio and ask her, "Why did you cut the ends off the ham before you put it in the oven?" She answered, "I never had a pan big enough to fit the ham in, so I had to cut the ends off."

Are you "cutting the ends off" because that's what you see everyone else doing? Are you living your life according to beliefs that are old and outdated? It doesn't have to be this way. You can break free from limited thinking and replace old ideas with new, life-enhancing beliefs. Limited beliefs and life experiences can keep you stuck and make you think you know everything, but none of us knows everything and no one ever will. The truth is that life has endless possibilities, not just the ones you can think of in your mind.

Your thinking is also limited by the people you choose to associate with. You probably chose your friends because they're like you. You could relate to them, they were "your kind of people," or you just "clicked." It feels good to be around people to whom you can relate. Unfortunately, if everyone you spend time with is the same as you, you create a reinforcement team that can help keep you stuck. You may fall into a tendency to commiserate about your problems but fail to come up with solutions. For example, Priscilla and Louise had been best friends virtually their entire lives. They had each divorced in their early forties and had some feelings of bitterness toward their ex-husbands. This commonality was comforting during the disruption of divorce proceedings, but eventually these friends realized they were doing each other more harm than good. They got into long discussions about how cruel their ex-husbands were and many times had discussions about how their were no decent men available. Their conversations kept them stuck in their past pain, making it difficult for them to move forward and find the new relationships they desired.

In *Love is Letting Go of Fear*, Gerald Jampolsky describes what happens when we stay in our comfort zone: "The mind can be thought of as containing reels and reels of motion picture film about our past experiences. These images are superimposed not only on each other but also on the lens through which we experience the present. Consequently, we are never really seeing or hearing it as it is; we are just seeing fragments of the present through the tons of distorted old memories that we layer over it." Sometimes our beliefs about how life is can cause us to slant events to fit our world view. For example, if we think, "I'll never get that job," or "This employer doesn't like me," we might misconstrue or slant the prospective employer's statements to prove ourselves right.

For example, a prospective employer will commonly say, "I have a few more interviews to conduct and I'll get back to you in a week." If we view this through the lens of our negative beliefs, we might say, "See, I knew she wouldn't like me." Many times an employer will give you the job if you call back. If you feel confident you might say, "Can I call you in a week to check in?" People who don't take the "I'll call you in a week" comment as a personal affront might get the job simply because they follow through. They also won't deal with the mental agony of wondering why the person doesn't like them or experiencing the fear of never finding a job.

If you want to see each day clearly and be open to the opportunities that they hold for you, you must first clear away the negative beliefs that cloud your vision. Stream of consciousness journaling or quiet times can help you identify some of these beliefs. As you do these activities, be sure to use the root down exercise and replace negative, unwanted beliefs with positive affirmations.

One of the challenges we must face if we want to expand our lives is to expand our thinking. We must go out on a limb and take action on our dreams even if they seem illogical and impossible, Even if other people tell us it can't be done. Risking means doing things that are extraordinary, expansive, new, and exciting. This is scary, but often times we will discover that our beliefs were the only thing that limited our lives. We may even be surprised someday that we ever could have believed those limitations in the first place.

We must take the words "I can't" out of our vocabulary and replace them with the words "it's possible." Begin breaking out of your comfort zone mentally by simply stating "it's possible" many times each day. This will open your mind to the way things are possible and send your mind on a mission to prove this belief right. In order to be free of limited thinking, you must let go of the need to "know" everything or the need to prove that you know everything, because that need kills ideas, creativity, and ingenuity. Biographies are filled with stories about people who became successful because they didn't "know" it was impossible. Let go of your "knowledge" for a minute and think with the enthusiasm of a child, be innocent, let your mind wander.

The Fun Way: Taking Risks

The greatest risk you can take is to be yourself and tell the truth. Sounds simple, yet few of us do it. Most of us live our lives based on rules and regulations. We live the life we think other people want us to live. A lot of the time we don't even know what we want because we've never stopped to figure it out. The biggest risk you can take is to acknowledge and dare to live your own dreams. Get to know who you really are and dare to be just that.

Another great risk is to feel your feelings, not those you think you should feel. You know you are fully alive if you laugh when you're happy, cry when you're sad, and scream when you're angry. In his book *Risking*, David Viscott writes, "The most important risk you can take is to be honest in expressing your feelings. If you do not express what you feel, you are forced to use defenses to keep unwanted feelings away. Whether you deny the feeling, justify it intellectually or pretend that it is unimportant, it is all the same. To the extent you do not experience your feelings, you do not experience the real world. Instead, the world you see becomes a creature created out of your needs, and your needs remain the product of feelings that have not been fulfilled."

The benefits of risking far outweigh the costs. Life has much in store for you and you have so much to add to life. Your creative ideas and inspirations are unique to you and life is waiting for you to act on your impulses. Carlisle often let perfectionism stand in the way of his success. His dreams included selling his photography to an art gallery and eventually publishing a book of his photos. He felt he wasn't good enough to accomplish this task and feared rejection from other artists. Carlisle was eventually persuaded to interview gallery managers and mentors in his field to get ideas of the direction he should be taking. Instead of rejection, Carlisle received support from other artists and was able to gleam valuable information that helped him get started in the field of photography. He was actually offered free advice and some of the artists he met spent hours of their time helping Carlisle compile a portfolio. He's further along in his goal than he could have imagined and is well on his way to achieving the objectives he set for himself.

Each step you successfully complete in the direction of your goal will make you stronger, better, and more confident.

When you are taking risks, you can expect to experience fear and insecurity. Sometimes this fear is so overwhelming, you may feel as if you are going to explode. You may come home from work crying every day, you may throw temper tantrums, you may raise your fist to God or the universe. All of that is normal. No matter how together someone may look on the outside, when they are on unfamiliar territory and taking a risk, they're going through the same feelings you are. They too feel like scared kids on the first day of school. But the good news is that risking gets easier every time you do it. Every time you walk through fear, you will become a little bit stronger. It's natural to feel uncomfortable when charting new territory, but the benefits of doing so far outweigh the costs.

Comments like "We love you just the way you are" may seem loving, but they can be a sign of sabotage from others. If you change, the people close to you have to change too, and maybe they don't want to. Your change may be a threat to them. Let's say you want to become more assertive and feel empowered. You will need to set boundaries and change the way you talk to people. Perhaps some people like you to be nonassertive so they can be in control and relate to you the way they're used to. Be aware of sabotage from others and push through it. Remember that you want to change, and that you have to look at yourself in the mirror every day. You might as well do what makes you feel best. Other people have their own resistance to deal with, but if you're persistent, they will get used to your change. In some cases you may need to call on a third party, such as a therapist or spiritual leader, for intervention. If you discuss others' resistance openly you should be able to discover ways to overcome them.

While you're changing and growing, you're having an effect on the people around you, especially those close to you. As you change, they have to change. Just as risk-taking gets easier for you each time you do it, others will adjust to your changes as time goes by. Don't give up because it seems like it's not worth it or it's too much trouble. If you make it through that difficult adjustment period, you will gain the courage and self-esteem to make it through the next time and the next time. Then, and only then, will your life become a great adventure rather than a ho-hum existence.

Walking through fear and discomfort can be seen as an exciting challenge, a daring adventure. Have fun with this time of your life. Know that if you stay strong, you will get all the rewards that life has to offer.

Task List and Action Plan

Before you go on to the next chapter, take time now to do these activities. They will help you get more out of the rest of this book.

- Imagine you have one month to live. What would be the most important thing to do?

- Make time for yourself each day.

- Write a lifeline that includes important life events. Extend the lifeline to the next twenty years. What would you like to see happen between now and then? Are you taking action to make that possible?

- As you look at your lifeline, see how events and people may have shaped your life and perceptions. Choose which life events you will continue to give power to and mark those that you want to perceive differently in the future.

- Write a list of times you let fear stand in your way. What were you afraid of? How can you overcome this fear in the future?

- List ten positive aspects of change. These are the points you will want to focus on every single day. Write them, read them, record them on a tape, and listen to them.

- Complete the breaking free worksheet.

Breaking Free

1. Three rules I live by are: _____

_____

_____

_____

These rules came from: _____

_____

_____

_____

2. The riskiest thing I ever did was: _____

_____

_____

Afterwards I felt: _____

_____

_____

3. One belief/opinion I have that is unpopular is: _____

_____

_____

I do share/don't share (circle one) this with others because: _____

_____

_____

4. The reasons I don't change are: _____

_____

_____

5. This keeps me comfortable because: _____

_____

_____

6. I could just as easily choose to: _____

_____

_____

11

Quitting Is the Only Way to Fail

Setbacks Are Part of Change

According to David Watson and Roland Tharp, we should expect setbacks and plan ways to deal with them in advance (1993). The book lists three of the greatest obstacles to change:

- You don't anticipate reasons for failure and cope with them.

- You don't believe you can change.

- You're ambivalent about changing.

They recommend dealing with these issues *now* in order to increase your chances of success.

As your life begins to change and you make forward progress, it's likely that you'll encounter setbacks. Setbacks are a natural part of change. Change usually happens in a three steps forward, two steps backward pattern. Feeling successful results from focusing on the steps forward, not the steps backward. Successful results come from continuous steps forward. Rather than using setbacks as an excuse to give up, use them as teachers to show you what's not working in your life and what needs to be changed.

If you view setbacks as learning experiences, you can devise a new plan of action to avoid repeated setbacks. If you view them as failures, you're more likely to quit. Rather than seeing a setback as complete failure, focus on what needs to be revised about your plan of action. What works? What doesn't work? Continue doing the things that work and analyze new approaches. Do something you haven't done before. Don't throw out your entire goal, just approach things from a slightly different angle.

There is a difference between a lapse and a relapse. Watson and Tharp define lapse as a brief return to undesired behavior and a relapse as a full return to your old habit. If you smoke a cigarette, you haven't blown your entire quit-smoking project, but if you go back to smoking a pack a day, you have. If you lapse and briefly return to undesirable behaviors, you can use this experience to gather information about which situations are most tempting and then formulate new ways to deal with them in the future. You have a choice to change at any time.

If you anticipate problems, you can decide how to deal with them in advance. Planning in advance for setbacks is like taking out an insurance policy. You may never need it, but it's nice to know it's there if you do. Take a moment to write out ways and reasons you're not succeeding. Then make goals to deal with these setbacks so they don't keep coming back. It's important to also write down what you're doing that's successful and keep this information for future reference. This way, when you get off-track, you can go back and look at what has been successful for you in the past and try it again.

Once you acknowledge that setbacks are part of change, and resistance doesn't make you a failure, you can anticipate it and have a plan of action to deal with it before it ever happens. For example, if you know that every time you try to quit smoking you automatically overeat, you can set up a way to deal with that in advance. Use some of the tools you've learned in this book such as positive self-talk, visualization, and practical goal setting.

One of the ways that perfectionism can stand in your way is that it leaves no room for errors. Yet setbacks and errors are part of changing and growing. Perfectionists don't want to consider setbacks. Setbacks don't fit into the unrealistic expectations of a perfectionist who wants total perfection all the time. Because of this all-or-nothing thinking, perfectionists are likely to drop an entire project because of one mistake rather than learning from the mistake and using it to help them succeed.

When you fail or make a mistake, it's a good opportunity to learn. Chances are, it isn't you that failed, it's the method you're using. If you have an open mind and self-acceptance, you can reevaluate your plan, mold it, and shape it until you come up with a custom-made success plan. If you give up at the first sign of defeat, you won't have this opportunity.

When you experience setbacks, review the techniques you've learned in this book. Have you committed to following them in your daily life? Are you taking time to be aware of what's standing in your way? Are you taking time to meditate, write in your journal, and do stress-reduction techniques to heighten your level of awareness? Are you using positive self-talk? Have you made an affirmation tape? Do you write in an affirmation journal? Are you saying affirmations daily? Are you focusing on and visualizing success? Did you make a beneficial billboard or self-fulfilling scrapbook? Are you writing in your creating history journal? Are your goals small and manageable, or have you set yourself up for failure by setting huge goals and feeling inferior because you haven't achieved them yet? Are you acknowledging and rewarding yourself regularly for the steps you've taken thus far? Are you moving out of your comfort zone and taking risks?

The techniques outlined in this book are designed to help you stay persistent and patient. All of the techniques work together, so if you're not doing one or more of them on a daily basis, ask yourself why. If you don't take new action and change old beliefs, you'll continue to get the same old results. Reevaluate your commitment and set a goal to use one of the techniques in this book today.

Chances are you already know some of the things that stand in your way of success. You've probably attempted self-change before. Why not make a list right now of new ways to deal with these obstacles in the future. Following is a list I've compiled from the responses of past workshop participants. Use it to help you identify the changes you want to make and list some of the reasons why you think you might not be able to succeed. You've probably attempted to change in these same areas more than once, so use information from the last time you attempted change to guide you in new directions. You may also want to return to your self-defeating attitude and behavior lists now and brainstorm some new ways to deal with these situations in the future.

Things That Might Make Me Want to Give Up	How I Will Deal With Them If They Occur
low self-esteem	I will use affirmations. I will find mentors and role models and know that if they can do it, so can I. I will not give up on myself.

family problems	I will set boundaries with my family. I know that I will be better able to take care of them if I take care of myself first.
money problems	I will reassess my financial situation. I will spend money wisely. I will write and stick to a budget. I will save money.
getting sick	I will care of my body by providing it with proper nutrition, plenty of sleep, and regular exercise. I will use positive affirmations and visualization to imagine myself healthy.
sabotage from others	Other people only have as much power as I give them. I will pay attention to my own inner voice. I won't concern myself with others' opinions.
moving out of town	Before I move to a new town, I will set up resources and get information that I need to succeed and feel supported.
negative thinking	I will use positive affirmations to drown out and change negative thinking.
self-doubt	I will make a list of all my accomplishments and read it daily. My past successes prove to me that I know how to succeed.
relationship problems	I will take responsibility for my part in the problems in my relationship with my partner. I will take all necessary steps before giving up and seek professional help and the support of others when needed.
lack of confidence	I will go out and do things that will make me feel more confident. I will use positive affirmations to boost my sense of self-esteem.
lack of motivation	I will start with something small and work my way up. I can do a little something today that will get me closer to my goals.
language barriers	I will work daily toward improving my language skills. I will spend time with people who can teach me how to move forward.
feeling unqualified	I will acknowledge the skills and talents I now possess, and I will improve upon them.

fear	I will remember that the only way to make a fear go away is to walk through it. I will do what I fear and watch fear disappear.
perfectionism	I will give myself credit for each step I take toward my goal, and I acknowledge that everything I do is a learning experience.
unrealistic expectations	I will change any self-defeating habits. I will give myself credit for all steps I take toward change.
"I can't do it"	I will realize the power of my own thinking. I know that when I tell myself I *can* do something, I *will* do it.
expectations from parents (parental pressure)	I can love my parents and myself at the same time. I am an individual and I dare to be myself. I will respect and nuture my individuality.
internal pressure	I will love and accept myself exactly as I am. I do not have to accomplish things to be lovable.
pressure to be a good parent	I will give love to my children and provide them with a positive role model as I show that it is okay to reach for your dreams and improve your life.

Here's a formula for problem solving that you can use to come up with alternatives to problems that haven't been listed as an example:

1. List the details of a problem or setback in your life. Keep a journal that details some of your observations as to why you didn't get the results you wanted.

2. Brainstorm solutions. Work with others, meditate, read, keep an open mind, write down all the alternative ways of thinking about and dealing with this situation.

3. Choose several solutions. Review solutions, and come up with the best one.

4. Implement the solutions. Devise a plan to take action. Be patient and persistent until you get the results you desire.

Winners Never Quit, Quitters Never Win

Calvin Coolidge once said, "Nothing in the world can take the place of persistence. Talent will not; nothing is more common than unsuccessful men with talent. Education will not; the world is full of educated derelicts. Persistence and determination alone are omnipotent. The slogan 'press on' has solved and always will solve the problems of the human race."

Three things that stand in the way of success are perfectionism, all-or-nothing thinking, and impatience. Although some changes happen more rapidly than others, long-lasting change takes time, energy, and work. Sometimes change occurs so slowly you don't feel like you're changing at all. No matter what happens or doesn't happen, *don't give up*! When you look closely at the successes of those around you, you will see that it took them time to get where they are now. If they can do it, so can you!

Beliefs are powerful. They shape our perceptions and expectations. Part of the reason they're so powerful is that we repeat them to ourselves day after day. We look for validation of our beliefs and they end up creating a self-fulfilling prophecy. Take a moment to think about how many years you've had negative, limiting self-talk. How many years have you rehearsed and reinforced self-defeating beliefs such as "I'll never get ahead," or "I'm not as good as other people," or "I don't have what it takes"? Compare the amount of time you've been thinking negative, limiting beliefs to the length of time you've been working on changing. If you've been living out the results of your old, outdated beliefs for twenty, thirty, forty, or fifty years and you've only worked on life-enhancing beliefs for a couple of weeks, months, or years, can you really expect to get instant results? You're working on changing things you've been doing for a long time, so it will take time to see progress. Permanent change happens very slowly, but it does happen. Chances are you're changing right now, even if you don't realize it.

Have you ever noticed how hard it is to pinpoint an exact moment in time when change occurred? You may not notice change while its happening, but that doesn't mean that it isn't. You may need to look back on where you were a year or two ago before you can realize that you are changing. When you make a conscious decision to change and put effort into doing so, it happens much quicker. If you continue taking the steps outlined in this book you will undoubtedly change.

Be patient with yourself. Keep the steps toward your goal small and manageable. If you fail to live up to your expectations, make your steps even smaller. Part of being patient with yourself means being patient with your self-change plan, even if it feels ridiculously easy and slow paced. Remember, success is what's important, not how quickly you attain it. You're working on permanent self-change, not a quick fix. Changing your behavior is just like learning to ride a bike or drive a manual transmission automobile—you get better with practice.

You may have heard the story of Thomas Edison. He "failed" ten thousand times before he invented a working lightbulb. When asked how he felt about this failure, he replied, "Why I haven't failed, I discovered ten thousand ways not to make a lightbulb." Michael Jordan wasn't even accepted to his high school basketball team. Was he a failure? No, because he used that setback and the discouragement he felt to strive harder, and he became one of the best basketball players in NBA history. Were they failures because they didn't get their success sooner? No, they would only have failed had they not continued to try.

Resting Isn't the Same as Quitting

There's a difference between resting and quitting. We all have times in our lives when things don't go as planned. We might find ourselves temporarily sidetracked from our goals and plans. Other times we just need a rest. If you "take off" for a day, a week, or even a month, that doesn't make you a failure. Diversion doesn't have to be permanent. As soon as things get back in order, you can begin focusing on your goal again.

It's self-defeating to quit just because you can't do things perfectly. Even when you have to temporarily postpone your goal, you can still use tools such as visualization and affirmations to stay on track mentally. These mental exercises can help open your mind to alternate solutions. You may not have to quit completely. You can reassess your schedule and priorities. You may find that although you cannot spend as much time as you had hoped, you can still do something. This will call for creativity on your part. Affirmations and visualization techniques learned in earlier chapters can help you handle these times more creatively.

By using affirmations that state your goal as being true right now or by visualizing your dream as being true right now, your mind goes to work to find a way to make it so. Even if you can't consciously figure out how to make things happen, there is a part of you that can, so let that part go to work for you during the times you are busy with other things. It's important to be flexible when you're working toward your goals. Sometimes what looks like a diversion or a setback in the beginning ends up showing you a new way to do things that's more efficient and satisfying in the long run. Sometimes the activities or people that divert us are really teachers in disguise, teaching us important skills that prepare us for upcoming success. So trust the process. Have faith that as your mental landscape changes, it will eventually influence your outside world.

Letting Go of Quick-Fix Mentality

We live in a society with quick-fix mentality. When we adopt this mentality for our personal philosophy, we lose. We're likely to buy things that are quick, easy, instant, and convenient, even if they don't work as well or aren't as healthy. Many times we pay more money for something that's quick and convenient because we value time and we want to do as many things as we can in as short a time possible. When it comes to personal development, however, quick fixes rarely lead to permanent change. When you're trying to learn a new way of doing something, it takes persistence and patience. Many people liken the mind to a computer, but computers are machines. They accept whatever information you give them. We, on the other hand, have feelings, thoughts, beliefs, morals, and codes that won't allow us to accept change without putting up a fight. It's to our advantage to drop the quick fix mentality and focus on long-term results.

Quick change is often a "false front." You may have heard stories of people who use affirmations and get instant results, but those results are likely to be temporary if the affirmations are not continued. If a person is not mentally prepared for success, they may let it pass them by as easily as it came to them. Perhaps they'll sabotage their success or find a way to create other problems in their life so they'll be distracted or have an excuse for not succeeding. True change will take more time, but it will last much longer.

Affirmations for Persistence

To help you develop a mental attitude of persistence, you may want to practice saying some of the following affirmations to yourself each day:

- I am persistent, and I go forward.

- I refuse to give up. I shall continue firmly, steadily, and insistently until my success appears.

- Winners never quit and quitters never win. I am a winner.

- It is my divine destiny to succeed, and it's God's business to help me. I expect and claim divine help now.

- The work of my hands and the plans of my life are now moving quickly toward a sure and perfect fulfillment. I anticipate the good. I now place my full trust in God/the universe.

- I am part of all that is good, and good shall be victorious.

- Every step I take I move closer to my goals.

- My goal is within reach. I continue moving forward.

Rehearsing and Practicing for Your Dream Life

When people want to excel in sports, music, art, theater, or dance, for example, they expect to spend time practicing on a daily basis. If you want to excel at life and stop settling and start living, you have a practice or rehearse daily. Imagine if you had an important part in a play and you wanted to do well. How many hours would you dedicate to perfecting your performance?

What if you wanted to compete in the Olympics? You would have to train mentally and physically for many years if you wanted to go for the gold. Isn't your life and happiness worth daily practice? Stop thinking of yourself as a person who is incapable of change and begin thinking of yourself as a person who is learning a new skill. Of course it will take time, but why not be alive and thriving rather than alive and existing? Remember the saying "Practice makes perfect," and think of yourself as someone who is practicing.

Commit to a Contract

One way to firm your commitment to change is to write out a contract with yourself and read it every day so you can keep focused. Fill out the contract at the end of this chapter. Then sign it, date it, and carry it with you. You might want to ask your friends or family members to help remind you of and support you in achieving your goal. Goal-group partners are the perfect people to share your contract with. Make sure that whoever you choose is trustworthy and loving and will not try to undermine your goal in any way.

Be flexible with the contract and allow yourself the luxury of "cheating" every once in a while. Remember, setbacks are a part of change, so expect them and accept them, and don't give them the power to detract from all of the positive changes you've made so far.

A written contract is a commitment you make to yourself that can help you remember what steps to take and why to take them. For example, if you're trying to work on assertiveness with a family member or friend, you could write a contract to yourself such as:

> I, __(your name)__ , am committed to my personal growth. The next time someone tries to tell me I can't succeed, I will repeat the following phrase to myself ten times, "I am competent and capable, I believe in myself." I will also be assertive when I feel I've been attacked or my needs aren't being met. When appropriate, I will say something like, "I really need your support. I would appreciate it if you help me stay positive." I will work toward setting boundaries and try not to take the comments of others personally.

After you make your contract, sign and date it. This helps make it feel more official. It can also help you in the future when you look back on it, allowing you to remember past struggles and gauge your progress. A sample contract form is provided for you at the end of this chapter.

If you have a contract in place before you need to use it, you will be better prepared to handle a difficult situation when it does come up. Reading your contract daily is a form of mental rehearsal that will prepare you to handle difficult situations if and when the need arises. You will have mentally prepared yourself, so you'll know what action to take. A contract is like an insurance policy. As you read it to yourself daily, you're preparing yourself to handle old events in a new way. You may never need the insurance policy, but it's a good thing to have. This way, a mishap won't demolish you, it will just give you a chance to readjust.

Keys to a Persistent Attitude

Many of the techniques in this book can help you gain an attitude of persistence. For example, creative daydreaming will help you keep a mental picture of your goals. It will also help to stay focused on taking small steps toward change and rewarding yourself for taking action. You should work continually to clear out any mental roadblocks to success. This might include alibis or excuses for your lack of success. Rather than believing limiting thoughts, examine them to see if they are really true. Look for exceptions to the rule and ways to get around roadblocks. Don't let outside circumstances stop you. Surround yourself with successful, inspirational people or read inspirational books about people who have overcome obstacles and roadblocks. Acknowledge that if they can do it, so can you.

When you encounter a roadblock, failure, or defeat, use it as a learning experience to see what needs to be changed. Take action every day, even if it's just working with your affirmations or looking at your beneficial billboard. Keep your mental focus on success. Be patient.

According to the book *Think and Grow Rich*, "Persistence is a state of mind, therefore it can be cultivated" (Hill 1972). The book outlines several attributes that can result in an attitude of persistence. These include definiteness of purpose, desire, self-reliance, definiteness of plans, accurate knowledge, cooperation, willpower, and habit. In order to develop persistence and patience, you must know what you want. Who wants to put intense effort and energy into something that's not important to them? Are you sure the goal you're striving for is your own? Strong desire comes from deep within your soul. It is based on your interests, talents, and priorities. Self-reliance is based on a belief in your abilities. Some of us have to build self-reliance from scratch. If you've never done anything on your own, you may not believe in yourself. Therefore, you'll sometimes have to act on faith or use your past successes in other areas or the successes of others as evidence that it can be done.

Definite plans can help you gauge your progress. If you don't have a map or a plan of how to get somewhere, you're more likely to get lost. If you don't know how to get to somewhere, get information from someone who has already been there. Search for the answer until you find it. You can get the accurate knowledge you need from a mentor or role model, someone who has been there and can help lead the way.

Napoleon Hill says the following about cooperation: "Sympathy, understanding, and harmonious cooperation with others tend to develop persistence." If you don't have these things in your life right now from the people you love, find other people to fill this need. You can join or start a support group so you can be surrounded by like-minded people.

Finally, use the power of your will to keep your focus on the end result you desire, rather than focusing on negativity and failure. Persistence can become a habit. The more you focus on success and take action toward your goals, the easier it will be to become persistent.

Task List and Action Plan

In order to get the most out of this book, take time now to do the action plan. Remember to keep up with all of the preceding steps. Whatever you do, don't give up!

- Use "Your Persistance Plan of Action" worksheet to write a list of the things that might stand in the way of your success. Then find a way to deal with them differently in the future. Ask for help from others if necessary.

- Do the commitment review worksheet that follows.

- Fill out the persistence inventory.

- Write an affirmation about persistence and say it to yourself daily.

- Write a contract based on persistence and patience and read it daily.

- Use information from the following worksheets to redirect your affirmations and goal setting.

Preparing for Success

1. What do you want to change and why? _____
_____
_____

2. What do you need to do to accomplish this change? _____
_____
_____

3. What are some of the reasons why you may not be able to accomplish this change?
_____
_____

4. What are some of the things that you think might stand in the way of your change? _____
_____
_____

5. What are some new ways you can deal with these obstacles in the future?
_____
_____

6. Write out affirmations to combat resistance. _____
_____
_____

Commitment Review

1. Are you aware of what is standing in your way? Yes or no? If yes, write it out.
_____
_____

If not, are you taking time out to meditate, journal and do stress reduction techniques to heighten your level of awareness? Yes or no? If no, why not? _____
_____
_____

2. Are you using positive self-talk? Yes or no?

When and how do you use positive self-talk? _____

_____

_____

Give an example of a time you used positive self-talk today: _____

_____

_____

Give an example of a time you used positive self-talk this week: _____

_____

_____

3. Have you made an affirmation tape or an affirmation journal? Yes or no?

4. Are you saying affirmations daily? Yes or no?

5. Are you focusing on and visualizing success? Yes or no?

6. Did you make a beneficial billboard or self-fulfilling scrapbook? Yes or no? If you have, do you look at it daily? Yes or no? If no, how often do you look at it?

_____

_____

7. Are you writing in your creating history journal? Yes or no?

8. Are you setting small, manageable goals so you don't set yourself up for failure? Yes or no?

_____

9. Are you rewarding yourself regularly for the steps you've taken thus far? Yes or no?

_____

10. Are you moving out of your comfort zone and taking risks? Yes or no? Give an example: _____

_____

_____

_____

Your Persistence Plan of Action

Use this worksheet to create a plan for success. Plan ahead how you will deal with setbacks.

Things That Might Make You Want to Give Up	How You Will Deal With Them If They Occur

Persistence Inventory

Use the following questionnaire to evaluate yourself and see where you can improve and make persistence a part of your life.

1. Do you have a clear picture of what it is you really want? If so, describe it below.

_____

_____

_____

_____

_____

_____

2. Do you know what you need to do to get there, or do you know someone else who does? If so, write it below. _____

_____

_____

_____

_____

_____

_____

3. Are you willing to take the necessary steps? Yes or no? Why? _____

_____

_____

_____

_____

4. Are you willing to persist at your goal even when it seems impossible? Yes or no?

_____

5. Are you willing to work toward your goal daily until it becomes natural to you? Yes or no? _____

6. Are you excited about attaining your goals? Do you look forward to attaining them? Yes or no? Why? _____

_____

_____

_____

_____

_____

7. Do you believe in yourself to use your knowledge and resources to your highest advantage? Yes or no? Why? _____

_____

_____

_____

8. Do you make excuses or alibis as to why you can't succeed? Yes or no? _____

9. What are your excuses and alibis? Are they valid? If so, why? _____

_____

_____

_____

_____

_____

_____

10. Do you blame your lack of success on outside circumstances? Yes or no? What are the circumstances? _____

_____

_____

_____

_____

_____

11. Can you change the outside circumstances? Yes or no? _____

    If no, why not? _____

    _____

    _____

    _____

    _____

12. Are you taking action to make your plans and dreams come true? Yes or no?
    If yes, please write below what you are doing. Be specific. _____

    _____

    _____

    _____

    _____

    _____

    _____

    _____

13. Do you have support from others? Yes or no? _____

    If so, who? _____

    _____

    _____

    _____

If no, have you attempted to form a support group? Yes or no? _____

14. Are you afraid of what others will think of you? Yes or no? _____

If so, what specifically frightens you? _____

_____

_____

_____

_____

_____

Self-Contract

Use the space below to write a self-contract. This is a commitment to yourself. It's your written statement of intention to change. A self-contract may start out something like this: "I, ___(your name)___ , commit to improving my health by letting go of my caffeine habit. When I feel an urge to drink caffeine, I will choose a decaffeinated drink instead, chew gum, call a friend, or review the positive aspects of change. I promise to do my best to fulfill the terms of this contract. However, if I fall off my contract, I will still give myself credit for my accomplishments and set out to accomplish my goal once more. I will not give up on myself no matter what until I have fulfilled the terms of this contract." Read this contract daily to remind yourself of your commitment.

_____

_____

_____

_____

_____

_____

_____

_____

_____

_____

_____

_____

Signed _____ Date _____

What Is Life Trying to Teach You?

Use this worksheet to help you realize how setbacks and trials can actually be used as learning experiences. Read the sample that follows, and then write about lessons you've learned from previous life experiences.

Event	What I Learned
got divorced after a brief marriage	It's important to listen to my intuition and be true to myself.
got fired from a great job	I need to communicate clearly and directly before I blow up. Forced me to look at other options and set me on a new career path.

Event	What I Learned

Now reevaluate a current struggle you're involved in:

Event	Possible Lessons

References

Amen, Daniel G. 1992. *Don't Shoot Yourself in the Foot*. New York: Warner Books.

Bradshaw, John. 1989. *Healing the Shame That Binds You*. Deerfield Beach, Fla.: HCI Audio Books.

Branden, Nathaniel. 1995. *The Six Pillars of Self-Esteem*. New York: Bantam Books.

Butterworth, Eric. 1983. *Spiritual Economics*. Unity Village, Mo.: Unity Books.

Chopra, Deepak. 1990. *Magical Mind, Magical Body*. Chicago: Nightingale Conant.

Frankl, Viktor. 1985. *Man's Search for Meaning*. New York: Washington Square Press.

Gawain, Shakti. 1978. *Creative Visualization*. Mill Valley, Calif.: Whatever Publishing.

Hay, Louise L. 1984. *You Can Heal Your Life*. Carson, Calif.: Hay House, Inc.

Hill, Napoleon. 1972. *Think and Grow Rich*. New York: Hawthorn/Dutton.

Jampolsky, Gerald G. 1979. *Love Is Letting Go of Fear*. Berkeley: Celestial Arts.

Jeffers, Susan. 1987. *Feel the Fear and Do It Anyway*. New York: Fawcett Columbine.

Lehrman, Fredrik. *Prosperity Consciousness*. Chicago: Nightingale Conant.

Rosenthal, Robert, and Lenore Jacobson. 1968. *Pygmalion in the Classroom: Teacher Expectation and Pupils' Intellectual Development*. New York: Holt, Rinehart, and Winston.

Schill, Thomas, Jane Beyler, Joann Morales, and Bonnie Ekstrom. 1999. Self-Defeating Personailty and Perceptions of Family Environment. *Psychological Reports* 69:744–746.

Sher, Barbara. 1979. *Wishcraft: How to Get What You Really Want*. New York: Ballantine Books.

Simon, Sidney B. 1989. *Getting Unstuck : Breaking through Your Barriers to Change*. New York: Warner Books.

Stephan, Naomi. 1994. *Fulfill Your Soul's Purpose: Ten Creative Paths to Your Life Mission*. Walpole, N.H.: Stillpoint Publishing.

Stevens, John O. 1971. *Awareness: Exploring, Experimenting, Experiencing*. Moab, Utah: Real People Press.

Swann, William B., Jr. 1996. *Self-Traps: The Elusive Quest for Higher Self-Esteem*. New York: W.H. Freeman and Company.

Viscott, David. 1977. *Risking*. New York: Pocket Books.

Vivano, Tamara F., and Thomas Schill. 1996. Relation of Reports of Sexual Abuse to Scores on Self-Defeating Personality Scale. *Psychological Reports* 79:615–617.

Watson, David L., and Roland G. Tharp. 1993. *Self-Directed Behavior: Self-Modification for Personal Adjustment*. Belmont, Calif.: Brooks/Cole Publishing.

Williams, Deirdre, and Thomas Schill. 1993. Attachment Histories of People with Characteristics of Self-Defeating Personality. *Psychological Reports* 73:1232–1234.

Ziglar, Zig. 1982. *Secrets of Closing the Sale*. New York: Berkeley Books.

Sheri O. Zampelli has been leading workshops on overcoming self-sabotage since 1992. She coaches private clients in successful goal attainment. Sheri ran the gamut of self-defeating behaviors, from drug addiction and homelessness to compulsive eating and procrastination, before finding the path to success. In *From Sabotage to Success* she reveals techniques that were essential to her own recovery and have helped thousands of others deal with this issue. For more information, visit Sheri's Web site at www.sabotagetosuccess.com.